CA

contemporary
architecture

Published in Australia in 2004 by
The Images Publishing Group Pty Ltd
ABN 89 059 734 431
6 Bastow Place, Mulgrave, Victoria, 3170, Australia
Telephone: +61 3 9561 5544 Facsimile: +61 3 9561 4860
Email: books@images.com.au
Website: www.imagespublishinggroup.com

ISSN 1447-8447
ISBN 1 920744 44 4

Co-ordinating Editor: Robyn Beaver

Designed by The Graphic Image Studio Pty Ltd, Mulgrave, Australia
Website: www.tgis.com.au

Film by Mission Productions Limited, Hong Kong
Printed by Everbest Printing Co. Ltd, in Hong Kong/China

Page 4 image of ABS House by Eric Sierins

images
Publishing

IMAGES has included on its
website a page for special notices
in relation to this and our other
publications. It includes updates in
relation to the information printed in
our books. Please visit this site:
www.imagespublishinggroup.com

CA

contemporary architecture

introduction by Catherine Slessor

The Australian Bureau of
Statistics assists and
encourages informed decision
making, research and discussion
within governments and the
community by providing a high
quality, objective and responsive
national statistical service

Contents

Introduction
Catherine Slessor

An intriguing and key theme of recent architecture has been the mainstream acceptance of the avant garde, of those designers with radical ideas who used to build little, but are now getting a chance to put their theoretical provocations into practice. On top of this, they are also now garnering recognition and acceptance from the architectural establishment, as witnessed by the awarding of the 2004 Pritzker Prize to Zaha Hadid and the 2003 RIBA Gold Medal to Rem Koolhaas. A decade or so ago, both were marginal figures in terms of built output, yet had an influence that belied this, seducing critics and potential clients with their unconventional approaches to space, form and materials. Bold architecture has always required imaginative patrons, and since then, a succession of institutions and individuals have provided the means and opportunity for these standard bearers of the avant garde to realise their distinctive visions.

Following the success of European projects such as a tram terminal in Strasbourg and a ski jump in Innsbruck, Zaha Hadid's new Contemporary Arts Center in Cincinnati marks her debut in the United States. In many ways, it also signifies her entry into the big league, being her first museum, and her first building to occupy a traditional urban site. Hadid is known for an architecture of gravity-defying expressiveness, but here, the energy is pent-up, the motion arrested. The CAC is designed from the inside out, as a three-dimensional jigsaw puzzle of galleries and offices on six levels above the street. The constant alternation of enclosure and void, the shifts of angle and level, the cutaways that reveal unexpected vistas, make for a sense of exhilaration that few art museums can match. As an urbane complex of galleries and gathering places, it challenges artists and curators to respond to the spaces and reshapes public perception of challenging works of art. Hadid looks outside architecture for her inspiration, to the realms of mathematics, which she originally studied, and cinematography, which underscores her restless, fractured, visionary paintings. Her 'paper architecture' has become her signature, both as finished art works and as a means of analysing relationships between space, materials and light. For Hadid, the act of drawing is a crucial, investigative process. Like many architects, she supplements traditional pen and paper renderings with technically sophisticated computer-generated images. New software programs have given her an intoxicating freedom to experiment with spatial and architectural concepts in ways that were unimaginable when she began her career. Paradoxically, her early hand-worked paintings, with their colliding, panning vistas of splintered buildings bear an uncanny resemblance to the now common currency of contemporary computer-generated presentations. Currently working on a new art museum in Rome and a station in Naples, Hadid's star continues to rise. The impression is that she has still to reach critical mass and her best work is yet to come.

Rem Koolhaas is also beginning to build more boldly and more extensively, with projects in Berlin for the Dutch Embassy, in which a labyrinthine ramp or 'trajectory' winds up and through the building, in Seattle (a new library) and in Porto, with a major new music theatre. This has been described as the city's equivalent of the Bilbao Guggenheim, in that it is a showpiece project by a foreign, superstar architect calculated to attract and stimulate cultural tourism. Drawn by the pace and ambitiousness of economic development in the Far East, Koolhaas is also making inroads into China, as are an increasing number of European and Western firms. His headquarters for Central Chinese Television (CCTV) will be among the first of 300 new towers to be constructed in Beijing's new Central Business District. China continues to modernise with astonishing and overwhelming rapidity, with its proportion of urban dwellers projected to rise from 35 to 60 per cent over the next ten years. This means that around 500 million more people will be living in Chinese cities. Boosted by a buoyant economy, growing at more than 17 per cent each year over the past decade, Beijing is currently a boom town and the staging of the Olympics there in 2008 has also helped to galvanise the country's architecture and planning. Swiss practice Herzog de Meuron has won a competition for the main National Stadium with a proposal that resembles a monumental bird's nest and Australian architects PTW are designing the National Swimming Stadium, which will be clad in an external skin of 'soap bubbles' (in reality inflatable pillows made of thin but immensely durable plastic film). Though China is seen as a growing market for

Western architects, the Chinese cannily encourage foreign firms to work with local partners in order to improve Chinese professional capabilities and design skills, so that they will not be endlessly reliant on outside expertise.

Major sporting events have always tended to provide a powerful incentive for urban development and set piece buildings (obvious examples being the Barcelona and Sydney Olympics, the recent World Cup in Japan and Korea and the Euro 2004 soccer tournament in Portugal), but other forms of public entertainment can also generate striking architecture. Such forms have generally required specialised buildings or sites that have evolved over time. Theatres, for instance, are one of the oldest types of urban architecture, embodying a human need for the rituals of public performance. Throughout history, the theatre has assumed many forms, reflecting the successive changes of images and identity that have occurred in the presentation of drama: the strolling player, the great open amphitheatre, the intimate court theatre, the proscenium frame, to contemporary remodellings of existing buildings and structures.

Beyond the insular tendencies of current

media technologies, there is still a fundamental need to make an experiential connection with art, performance, space, place and the wider world. Among recent projects for entertainment that make and sustain this connection are Renzo Piano's new concert hall in Parma which creates a lively new civic forum, and Mansilla + Tuñon's theatre in Léon which provides a sophisticated setting for classical music but also has bold urbanistic ambitions. Mansilla + Tuñon began their careers in the office of Rafael Moneo and their work displays similar formal preoccupations that have their roots in traditional Iberian architecture tempered by a Modernist restraint. Neutral, toplit containers, solid, alcazar-like walls and the subtle play of light are intelligently choreographed to create a sense of depth and solidity. All this is underscored by material refinement and concern for how things are made and put together.

The bulk of Léon's new concert hall is essentially a blind box clad in crisp white travertine, but on the edge of the square, the box cranks round abruptly to terminate in a massive wall that addresses its neighbours, like some kind of three-dimensional billboard, adding a new piece to the existing urban composition. A grid of deeply recessed and splayed bays containing windows of different sizes captures small chasms of light which cast changing reflections and pockets of intense luminosity through the spaces inside, echoing the way in which light percolates through the thick walls of Spanish churches. In fact in its solidity, whiteness, and geometric play of shadows, the wall is a dramatic abstraction of Iberian vernacular architecture, so that the new theatre sustains and builds on a connection with the past.

A continent away, Frank Gehry's new Walt Disney Concert Hall in Los Angeles has finally been completed, providing the city with a major new cultural and urban focus. Instantaneously acclaimed as a vanguard masterpiece, its giant external petals of stainless steel cladding form exotic new landmarks among the isolated towers of downtown Los Angeles. From afar, they glisten and reflect the sky, then taunt and swoop away when viewed up-close, like the cape of a demented matador. Though Gehry still begins each project with hand-made models, his exploration of complex new geometries is made possible by increasingly sophisticated computer programs; Disney Hall is no exception. Inside, the 2,265-seat auditorium is lined or draped in timber, evoking further analogies – the inside of a ship's hull or like being in a musical instrument itself. In their different ways, these projects illustrate the relationship of people to place and how spaces for entertainment can help to civilise and enrich the urban realm. Yet cities are also places for a diverse range of activities, from working and learning, to socialising and shopping. An increasingly important factor in the future growth and development of urban centres is the creation of diversity in both buildings and neighbourhoods; easy to theorise about, but often difficult to achieve in practice.

Until the railways and, more recently, the car put physical distance between people and their places of work, education, worship and entertainment, the texture of towns was often astonishingly rich, sustaining a much greater number and range of functions than contemporary dormitory villages or dead city centres. In the twentieth century however, population growth and increased car ownership have fuelled the expansion of homogeneous suburbs and out-of-town centres for shopping and leisure. This easy-to-implement but highly wasteful model of development is still in the ascendancy over a more complex idyll of high density, less vehicle-fixated, variegated, urban communities.

Yet the continued growth of suburbs and dependence on private transport is clearly not sustainable. In Detroit, for instance, where the flight to the suburbs has emptied the city's heart, petrol consumption is nine times that of Copenhagen, where a greater number of people live in the centre. Politicians and planners now accept that all new development cannot be accommodated by greenfield sites or new towns; some must go back into cities, often in areas previously used for commerce or industry. After the acknowledged social and environmental failure of Modernist planning, which promulgated a brave new world structured around tidy zones of single use, efforts are now being made to rekindle the vitality and improve the viability of urban centres through the active encouragement of greater diversity. Urban designers have long supported mixed use as an essential component of successful cities, providing the foundations for lively, safe and stimulating neighbourhoods.

Some examples of how diversity can generate more rewarding and humane architecture range from Nicholas Grimshaw's revitalisation of Bath Spa, in which a precious historic structure is sensitively repaired and adapted for a range of modern uses, to Lab Architecture's Federation Square development in Melbourne which, in spite of its fashionably fragmented approach to form making, brings together a mixture of functions intended to animate the city centre. Such projects demonstrate what can be achieved with vision and persistence to improve the quality of urban life.

The encouragement of mixed use development in cities forms part of a wider debate on sustainability, which continues to preoccupy many leading architects. In general, the emergence of sustainability as a recognisable movement is clearly to be welcomed, for it offers the prospect of a holistic response to the present environmental crisis and makes much-needed connections between nature, culture, economics, politics and technology. The first generation of ecological or sustainable design to evolve following the energy crisis of the mid-1970s was based on tentative, small-scale experiments, with new technologies and ideas adopted in a piecemeal fashion. Now this is changing, as current generations of architects and designers learn to integrate the insights of a range of disciplines and foster an ecologically responsive approach to planning and building.

Architects have always been known as generalists, capable of assimilating a wide variety of information and converting it into a solution. Sustainability challenges that ability as it encompasses areas as diverse as ethics, economics, sociology, ecology, history and biology. The analytical and deductive skills of architects can be used to make sense of the complex systems and interactions of global ecology. There is hope that the profession can become instrumental in providing research to guide and stimulate change. Many practices are showing the way, especially in Germany, where more stringent building and planning regulations actively encourage green architecture.

Behnisch, Behnisch & Partner's recently completed headquarters for Entory AG, for instance, extends the practice's long and distinguished lineage of humanely conceived, environmentally responsive workplaces. With its predominantly permeable aspect and office wings reaching into the landscape, Behnisch's scheme responds sensitively to its setting and engages with its surroundings. Two five-storey volumes are arranged in a rough L-shape around a fulcrum of foyer spaces and a staff canteen, but floors are pushed and pulled in the manner of desk drawers sliding in and out and over and under each other. The characteristic layering of the façades and use of colour enhances the spirit of animated bricolage, breaking up the building mass and subverting notions of corporate decorum. External blinds shade and screen the glazed envelope and subtly coloured cladding made of a special translucent, photosensitive material change hue with changing light, like strips of chameleon skin.

Inside, offices are conceived as distinct places, rather than arid, impersonal prairies, with cellular and open plan spaces interspersed to create a varied and changeable internal landscape. In terms of energy use and environmental control, the building is equally responsive to its users' needs, employing a system based on the principles of thermal mass, natural ventilation and water-borne radiant cooling and heating delivered via plastic pipes cast directly into concrete ceilings. Compared to a similarly sized building, Entory's architects and engineers predict that its energy consumption will be considerably reduced, but its success, as with other Behnisch office projects, also lies in the way it humanises and civilises the environment of the corporate workplace. As a building type, offices might not normally be associated with ecological awareness, but there are signs that environmentally responsive architecture has at last progressed beyond the domestic scale to play a more meaningful role in the wider, corporate world. New headquarters for Telenor, the leading Norwegian telecommunications company, designed by American practice NBBJ give some sense of how this is being achieved. Despite housing a workforce of 6,000, Telenor emphasises the human scale, through informal planning that encourages employee interaction. Abundant natural light and ventilation, frugal use of artificial lighting, and a net surplus on energy use, also make the building an impressive model of sustainability. In both organisational and environmental terms, Telenor is an inspiring glimpse of the future that will hopefully exercise a persuasive influence on other forward-looking corporations.

From an office campus in Oslo to a new tower in the heart of London, exciting new paradigms are being created for large-scale green architecture. In its new building for Swiss Re, Foster and Partners has produced one of London's largest office buildings, which apart from being an iconic addition to the skyline in its distinctive cigar-shaped form, suggests new possibilities for environmentally aware high-rise development. Built on the site of the former Baltic Exchange, the 40-storey tower joins the cluster of tall buildings that symbolises the heart of London's financial centre.

Spatially, socially and environmentally it explores a radical agenda for a building of its type, with structure, form and fabric ingeniously integrated. An especially striking feature is the use of enclosed lightwells inside a double-skinned energy-efficient façade. Spiralling on a 5-degree rotation for each floor up the building, the lightwells not only bring daylight into the core but also assist natural ventilation through openable windows in the external membrane. Achieving natural ventilation proved a significant impetus in refining the building's form and skin, which was extensively modelled and wind-tunnel tested. As a result, it is anticipated that the tower could be naturally ventilated for at least 40 per cent of the year, setting a benchmark for new commercial developments.

Foster's new tower takes its place in the heart of the City of London, historically the oldest part of metropolis and now its business district. Here, a skyline of gleaming office towers looms incongruously over a dense network of streets and historic churches, many designed by Christopher Wren when the City was reconstructed following the Great Fire of London in the seventeenth century. Though this visual paradox aptly reflects the triumph of worldly concerns over the spiritual, the recent completion of Rafael Moneo's new cathedral in Los Angeles and Richard Meier's church in Rome recall a time when faith was a powerful force in shaping the built environment. Today, human existence is predominantly secular, with religion seen as a futile and slightly nonsensical pursuit. Yet despite currently occupying the margins of contemporary life, religion, mythology and ritual are still fundamental aspects of human consciousness.

Before the modern age, religion and daily existence were essentially inseparable and there was little distinction between the spiritual and the secular. Even with the benefits bestowed by intellectual and technological progress, much of our social behaviour originates in the past and the human psyche has been immutably shaped by preceding generations. As in other areas of culture, architecture embraces and appropriates ancient rites, though often unconsciously.

Groundbreaking ceremonies for new buildings symbolically consecrate the site, and the act of topping out marks the completion of the superstructure by attaching a sprig of pine to its tallest point, symbolising rebirth and regeneration. Religion and myth have long served as a means of explaining the world and our place within it. The creation of belief systems provided answers to questions of existence and reinforced a crucial sense of security in hostile physical and social environments. Architecture serves a similar purpose, transcending function to respond to symbolic needs and expressing meanings associated with human existence at its deepest and most fundamental level. Religious beliefs are made manifest by rituals and ceremonies that are generators of a bewildering multiplicity of architectural forms, from the monumental stupas of Buddhism to Christian churches.

What then, of making architecture that connects with the divine in today's transient, secular society? With the dissolution of dogmatic certainty, ecclesiastical commissions are no longer a corset of liturgical convention, but an opportunity for freedom of expression. Such autonomy invariably reflects the technical and aesthetic concerns of individual architects; for instance, Rafael Moneo's sumptuous alabaster walls that seem alive with light in LA's new Catholic cathedral, Richard Meier's serene orchestration of space in Rome, and Renzo Piano's massive stone arches that articulate his huge pilgrimage basilica in Puglia, in southern Italy. But within this difference in approach, it is still possible to discern and experience moments of inexplicable resonance – the touch of stone, the flicker of light, the gathering of souls – that express the human desire to commune with forces more venerable and mysterious than the cosmos itself. In the current global climate of uncertainty and instability, architecture in all its forms can still act as a powerful force for transcendence and enlightenment.

Catherine Slessor

Corporate

30 St Mary Axe
Swiss Re UK Headquarters, London, UK
Foster and Partners

The capital's first environmentally progressive tall building, 30 St Mary Axe is not only an office building; its street level is publicly accessible with double-height retail outlets serving the local working community, and the building is set within a new public plaza.

The 40-storey tower has a circular plan that widens as it rises from the ground and then tapers towards its apex. Mid-height, the floor-plates offer large areas of office accommodation; the tapering apex of the tower minimises the extent of reflected sky. The aerodynamic form encourages wind to flow around its face, minimising wind loads on the structure and cladding, enabling the use of a more efficient structure. Wind deflection to ground level is greatly reduced, helping to maintain pedestrian comfort and safety at the base of the building.

The building can utilise natural ventilation in addition to air conditioning, so that for up to 40 per cent of the year, much of the mechanical cooling and ventilation supply systems can be supplemented, reducing energy consumption and carbon dioxide emissions. Fresh air may be drawn through lightwells, which spiral up the building, to ventilate the offices naturally. The lightwells are clad with simple operable and fixed double-glazed panels with tinted glass and a high-performance coating, maximising daylight penetration to the office areas and reducing reliance on artificial lighting.

The 180-metre-tall (600-foot) tower is supported by a highly efficient structure consisting of a central core and a perimeter diagrid – a grid of diagonally interlocking steel elements. Because of the inherent stiffness of the external diagrid, the central core is required to act only as a load-bearing element and is free from diagonal bracing, producing more flexible floor plates.

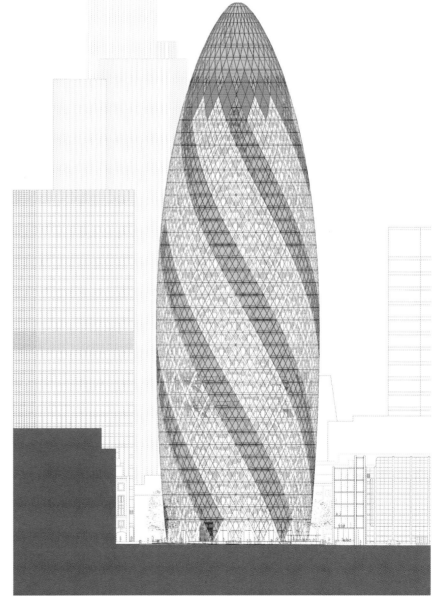

completion	2003
client	Swiss Re
area	46,000 square metres/500,000 square feet (net office area)
	1,400 square metres/15,000 square feet (net retail area)
structure	Steel, concrete
materials	Glass cladding with aluminium profiles
opposite	General view
top	Panoramic view of London skyline from River Thames
bottom	Elevation
photography	Nigel Young

Chesapeake Fitness Center
Oklahoma City, Oklahoma, USA
Elliott + Associates Architects

The program required the largest possible building volume on a limited site to house a corporate campus fitness centre. The exterior of the new structure was required to maintain the modified Georgian architecture to match the existing campus, but with a modern interior and state-of-the-art facilities. The management goal is to use the fitness centre to increase staff well-being, and as a recruitment tool to attract high quality staff.

The goals for the architectural concept included: provision of excellent acoustics in normally reverberate spaces like swimming pools, gymnasiums and locker rooms; the introduction of natural light into spaces like the swimming pool and gymnasium that normally do not have windows; the introduction of spatial drama, great lighting, high quality materials, art, and music to create a memorable atmosphere and thus enhancing the centre as a marketing and recruitment tool for the company; the creation of outdoor spaces for walking/jogging and volleyball; provision of an outdoor courtyard including a barbeque cooker and fire pit for outdoor events; and the creation of a compatible and mutually supportive relationship between the architecture and the interior uses.

Interior functions include entry lobby and check-in, 25-metre swimming pool with men's and women's locker rooms, racquetball, squash and basketball courts, weight, cardio and aerobics rooms, offices, children's area, tanning salon and support areas.

completion	May 2003
client	Chesapeake Energy Corporation
area	3690 square metres/39,688 square feet
awards	AIA Oklahoma Design Excellence Award
	25th Annual Interiors Award, sponsored by *Contract* magazine
opposite	View from pool looking north at hot tub on right and upper level entry
top	North–south section
bottom	Gymnasium looking south; note skylights and window steel protection screen
photography	Robert Shimer, Hedrich-Blessing

COoP Editorial
Santa Monica, California, USA
Pugh + Scarpa

The design of this tenant improvement evolved from the unique challenge to remodel a 1963, Frank Gehry-designed commercial structure located in the heart of downtown Santa Monica.

The design examines the tension between materials, form and experience. The interior can be viewed as 'a skin or surface wrapper that moves in and out alternately concealing and revealing the building fabric'. The layering and sculpting of the newly formed surfaces weave together disparate and contrasting materials.

Of particular interest is the idea of transcending traditional craft and elevating humble materials without trying to make them into something other than what they really are. The exploration encourages the user to forge a deeper and more meaningful understanding of the fundamental, yet delicate relationships that exist between themselves, the natural world, its vital resources, and our collective cultures.

Two basic materials, wood and plastic, are transformed from benign surfaces into sculpted space. The 100-foot-long wood wall was created by a direct transfer method. Computer models were sent directly from the architect to a computerized CNC router where 74 glue-laminated beams of varying thickness were sculpted by direct automation. The result is a surface that is spatial, has depth and comes alive with movement.

In contrast to the carving method of the wood construction, coloured acrylic panels were layered to a thickness of one inch for the façades of the adjacent lead-lined offices. The panels are backlit from large skylights located within the interior of their respective offices and are transformed into a material of considerable spatial depth and colour.

By placing objects and materials 'outside the frame', a new frame of reference deepens our sense of perception. Art does not reproduce what we see; rather it makes us see.

completion	May 2003
client	Optimus Corporation
area	437 square metres/4700 square feet
cost	USD$410,000
awards	Record Interiors 2003
	American Institute of Architects LA Honor Award 2003
	American Institute of Architects National Design Award 2003
opposite	Back-lit layered acrylic walls and a 100-foot CNC wall surround the public space
top	Looking toward main entry and conference room
bottom	Detail of reception area looking towards kitchen
photography	Marvin Rand

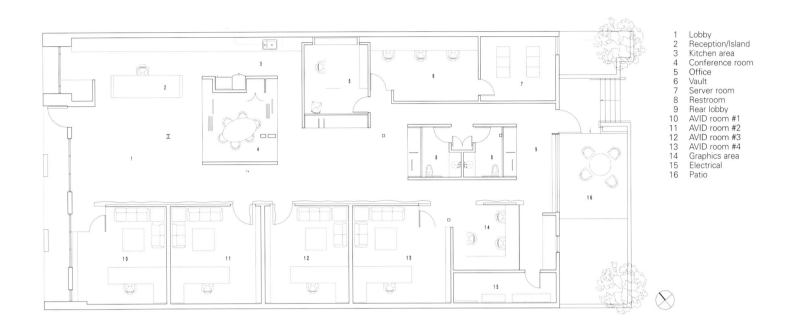

1	Lobby
2	Reception/Island
3	Kitchen area
4	Conference room
5	Office
6	Vault
7	Server room
8	Restroom
9	Rear lobby
10	AVID room #1
11	AVID room #2
12	AVID room #3
13	AVID room #4
14	Graphics area
15	Electrical
16	Patio

top	Ground floor plan
right	Layered acrylic wall panels around studio sitting area
bottom	Detail of CNC wood wall
opposite	Conference room looking toward studio sitting area
photography	Marvin Rand

Entory Home

Ettlingen, Germany
Behnisch, Behnisch & Partner

The site of 'Entory Home', Entory AG's new headquarters, was previously occupied by a military barracks at the northern periphery of Ettlingen, near the access roads to the city centre. It affords views of surrounding meadows and the soft, rolling hills of the Black Forest.

The client needed a building with a variety of different spaces suitable both for teamwork and individual work, as well as the capability to adapt to future working modes of its approximately 350 employees. In addition, spaces were to be created where people can conveniently meet, communicate and exchange information, thus strengthening the feeling of 'belonging together.'

The new headquarters were designed as a corporate 'home' in every sense of the word. Visually, the building is a signature Behnisch, Behnisch & Partner form – sleek, beautiful geometry in the form of raised masses with sensitive water elements and landscaping – but with a series of provocative, tailor-made variations.

The building is a series of rising, slab-rectangles of varying size, set at 90 degrees to each other. These masses appear apart, yet together; various streaming movements meet at different levels. Poles raise each mass to a different level, enabling their ends to project out above the underlying form. Cantilevered decks and skylights punctuate each mass; with the top one featuring a long, narrow roof slab seemingly sliced out of the rectangle itself. Fenestration space divides the masses horizontally near their flat roof-lines, creating the illusion of slim rectangles hovering above the main ones.

The building rests on 150 thermally functional, sunken reinforced concrete piles. During the winter months, water circulated through coiled piping laid within the piles and warmed by the earth is, in conjunction with the pipework laid in the concrete floor plates, used for heating purposes. Windows in all rooms can be opened for natural ventilation.

completion   2003
client   LVM Lebensversicherungs-AG
area   10,845 square metres/116,700 square feet
opposite   Restaurant is oriented towards garden
top   Cantilevered decks punctuate mass forms
bottom   Skylights slit across entrance atrium ceiling
photography   Christian Kandzia/Behnisch, Behnisch & Partner

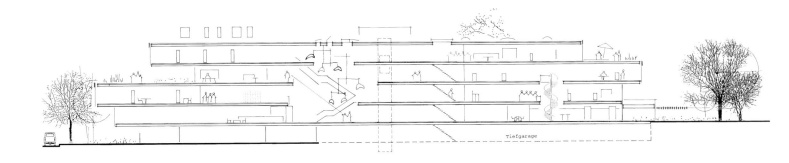

opposite top	Section shows areas for casual meeting
opposite middle	'Spanish stair' entrance to atrium
below	Entory glows with colour, inside and out
bottom	Architects respond to the rural setting
photography	Christian Kandzia/Behnisch, Behnisch & Partner

L'Oréal Headquarters
Brussels, Belgium
ASSAR

Located in the Erasmus Scientific Park in suburban Brussels, this low-rise project has been designed to house the three divisions of L'Oréal in Belgium and Luxembourg. The curved building allowed a large surface area on a restricted site.

The 'L' and 'O' in the L'Oréal name inspired the typical floor plan. Of more importance, the floor plan allows the harmonious integration of the three L'Oréal components in three different areas, each with its own vital core. Each product division is located on a separate level while each level offers specific areas such as offices or a training centre at the same location.

It was important that the project reflected the high-profile international corporate and brand image of the L'Oreal name. The curved façade creates a vivid moving architecture without unnecessary ornamental features. Another fundamental goal was to enhance daily communication between people who were previously housed in different locations in the city. All emergency staircases are inviting and user-friendly, encouraging their daily use – this has in fact almost eliminated the use of the elevators in the building. The transparent, well-lit staircases allow those passing by a glimpse of the internal working of the company. The project has been designed to allow visitors to walk through all public spaces (such as the atrium, reception area, training centre, restaurant, and garden terrace), without the need of passing through the security checkpoint that employees have to pass through to access their own restricted working environments. At the same time, employees can move around the atrium and the public zone without encountering guests and visitors. The architect of the L'Oréal Headquarters building was also responsible for two adjacent projects – the UCB World Headquarters and Sopres – allowing the creation of a coherent ensemble of buildings.

client	IDIM
completion	July 2002
area	18,500 square metres/200,000 square feet
structure	Prefabricated concrete
materials	Granite, structural glazing melted on stainless steel structure
opposite top	General view with main entrance access
opposite bottom	Night view
photography	Marc Detiffe
top	Main elevation
photography	Philippe Doutrèwe
middle	Main entrance access
bottom	Façade detail
photography	Marc Detiffe

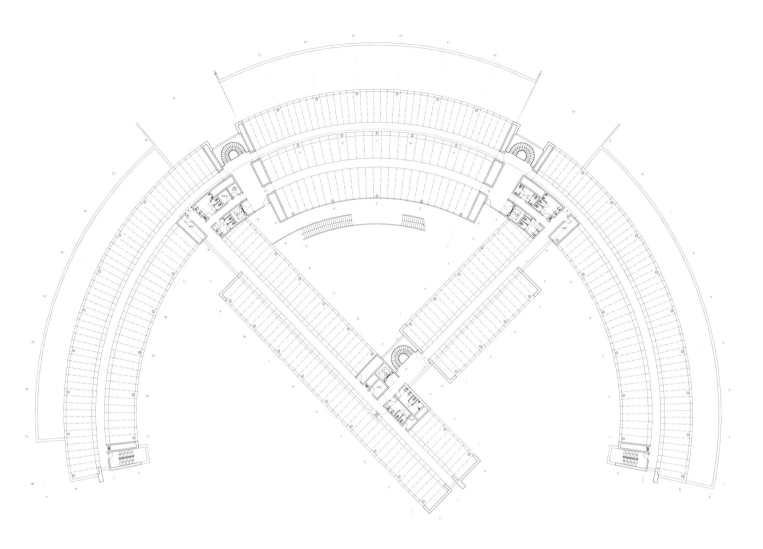

opposite top   Typical floor plan
opposite bottom, right and bottom left   Atrium views
bottom right   Glass-enclosed staircases
photography   Marc Detiffe

Noevir USA
Irvine, California, USA
space international inc.

Nature and technology merge in this corporate showroom and offices for a Japanese cosmetics company. The ground floor conversion of an existing concrete tilt up warehouse called for a transformation of the harsh industrial shell to accommodate a serene setting for the company's display line of 'scientifically engineered natural beauty products'. A combination of natural and artificial materials is used in a cooperative metaphor for the scientific nature of the space, each accentuating the intrinsic relationship between surface and volume, interior and exterior, program and form. A translucent laminated glass curtain wall drapes the interior perimeter, veiling views of the industrial landscape through a series of slotted apertures. The raised terrazzo showroom floor frames monolithic display tables of acrylic polymer, which float on translucent acrylic columns. A layered band contains the reception and service areas, separating the retail area from the offices behind. Limestone-clad walls and floors accentuate the remaining programmatic volumes such as the conference room, café/lounge area and skin-care salon.

Set in a manufacturing complex that also serves as the company's North American distribution facility, the main challenge of the project lies in attempting to create a serene, spa-like atmosphere in the centre of a chaotic industrial environment. This situation reveals that the dialectic between 'natural' and 'artificial' environments is not perfectly clear, but rather, 'clearly ambiguous'.

completion	February 2002
client	Noevir USA, Inc.
materials	Honed limestone flooring and walls; microterrazzo flooring; walnut, Corian and acrylic millwork; white and clear laminated glass
awards	11th Annual IIDA Will Ching Award 2003 Dupont Benedictus Awards, Honorable Mention *Contract* magazine 25th Annual Interiors Award
opposite	View of showroom highlighting main product display table; dual-laminated glass curtain wall in background buffers the private offices beyond
top	Architectural volumes interlock spatially to veil relationships between private and public functions such as salon and conference room
bottom	Monolithic display tables floating above highly reflective floor are supported by translucent acrylic columns
photography	Benny Chan, fotoworks

opposite   View along perimeter display towards limestone-clad conference room partition, hovering lightly over floor

top   Laminated glass curtain wall surrounds interior perimeter of showroom, creating a variety of spectral effects through mitigation of natural light

above   Built-in window seat at reception spans upper and lower floor levels

photography   Benny Chan, fotoworks

Ocala Electric Utilities Facility
Ocala, Florida, USA
Architects Design Group, Inc.

This administrative facility was designed to serve the functions of customer service, management, finance, public affairs, contract compliance and auditing for the Electric Utility Company of Ocala, Florida. Architects Design Group, Inc. was selected among other highly technical firms to create a more efficient facility with future expansion capabilities, resulting in an innovative and environmentally responsive workplace.

ADG accomplished the client's goals first by creating a lightweight structure with solar shading, resulting in a 30 per cent lower rate of energy consumption than the Florida energy efficiency requirements for this type of building. Other environmentally cautious features include day lighting with the appropriate use of high-performance glazing systems, the careful layout of interior open plan work areas and natural lighting to reduce artificial light levels. This simple, yet functional design was completed with a highly insulated stucco finish and a white reflective single-ply membrane roofing system. Each of these factors utilised sustainable technologies adapted to an understanding of Central Florida's unique, subtropical climate.

completion	August 2003
client	Ocala Electric Utility Company
area	2695 square metres/29,000 square feet
structure	Reinforced concrete and steel framing
materials	Stucco on masonry; exposed structural steel
awards	2003 American Institute of Architects Orlando Chapter Award for Design Excellence
opposite top	Entrance to facility
opposite bottom	View toward plaza
top	Light monitors at upper level
bottom	Electronic payment units in lobby
photography	Kevin Haas

Pharmacological Research Laboratories

Biberach, Germany
sauerbruch hutton architects

The building, which is part of the research campus of the pharmaceutical firm Boehringer Ingelheim Pharma KG, accommodates mainly laboratories and offices.

The long, seven-storey structure follows a predetermined building envelope, which facilitates its direct architectural and functional connection to an existing adjacent building. The spacious ground floor foyer is a unifying element that brings together the various routes traversing the campus. As well as being used as the main entrance, the foyer houses a cafeteria and smoking areas, and can also host informal lectures.

The rest of the building is structured into three parts: a naturally ventilated office area on the west side; an air-conditioned and naturally lit laboratory zone with its elaborate installations to the east; and a 'dark' zone containing highly serviced special rooms.

An atrium between the main zones admits daylight deep within the building. It also acts as a convection space, promoting natural ventilation in the offices. In the summer, this area will be cooled naturally using night air, the large surfaces of exposed concrete providing good thermal mass. An open staircase within the atrium directly connects the various levels.

The outer skin of the building comprises two layers – the inner skin that acts as a traditional fenestrated wall; and the outer skin, composed of vertical glass louvres that, as well as providing sun shading, unite the building's diverse parts into a unified whole. This colourful and idiosyncratic façade makes a lively, contemporary and striking impression which symbolises the quality of research at this location.

The skin is also 'intelligent' as it regulates external climatic influences – each façade is individually controlled, and the louvres are able to track the sun on its path during the day. The thermal performance of the building is optimised through a central building management system.

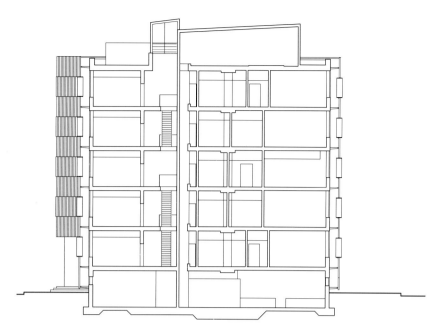

completion	October 2002
client	Boehringer Ingelheim Pharma KG
area	10,600 square metres/114,100 square feet
structure	Reinforced concrete
materials	Inner façade is clad with exposed insulation material, outer of single pane tempered glass with a silk-screened fret
cost	EUR17.25 million
awards	RIBA Awards 2003
opposite top	West façade, night view
opposite bottom	View from southeast
top	Section C
bottom	West façade with louvres in open position
photography	Gerrit Engel

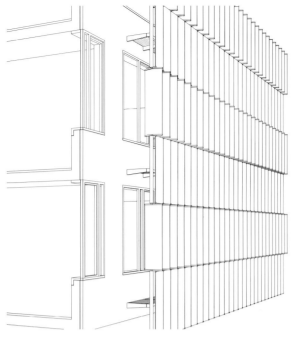

opposite   Closeup view from southeast
top   Façade perspective
right   Closeup view from southwest
bottom   First floor plan
photography   Gerrit Engel

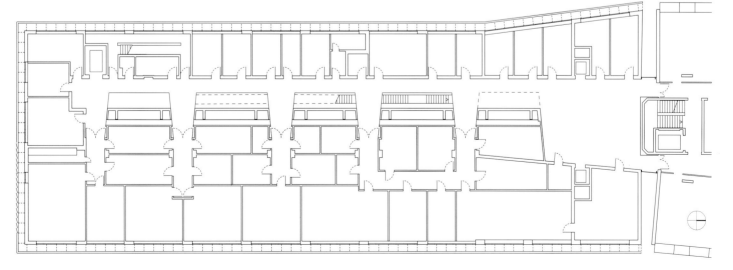

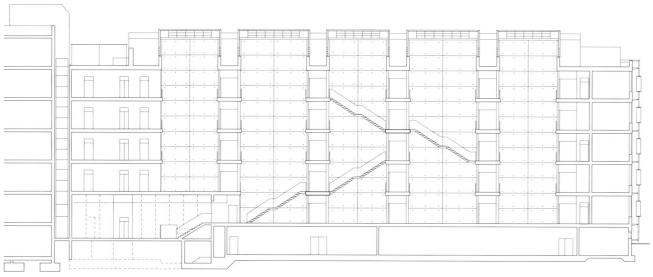

top   Entrance hall
bottom   Longitudinal section A
opposite   Atrium
photography   Gerrit Engel

Post Tower
Bonn, Germany
Murphy/Jahn, Inc.

The Post Tower represents a new typology for an office tower. The north and south halfshells are separated by 7.2-metre-wide spaces, which are divided at 9-storey interval floors by glass-floored sky-gardens, which also serve as communication floors. At the top, a 2-storey space and a penthouse with a screened roof terrace define the executive areas. Two groups of glass elevators serve all floors and allow dramatic views of the city and the landscape.

The façade is adaptable and switchable. Natural ventilation, daylight with its connected solar energy and their intelligent control are the main strategies.

The interior follows the typical German standard of a cellular office layout. By designing a special glass partition system, which is now available on the market, the goals of visual openness and transparency have been achieved through clear and translucent surfaces, which also meet the occupants' need for privacy.

Lighting and lighting art are integral parts of the architecture. The functional office lighting and the façade lighting vary with the occupancy of the building and result in dynamic colour variations.

All structural elements of the main buildings as well as the façade have been designed to achieve maximum lightness, transparency and clarity. Many parts of the structure are multifunctional; for example, the slabs that act as structural elements, basic heating/cooling devices and as light reflectors.

'Breathing in the wind' describes the balanced airflow through the different façade layers and spaces. The building is ventilated year-round through the air space between the shells without using the central mechanical system. The comfort and energy concept is controlled by the individual user with regards to the space temperature, air quality and room illumination.

As a result of the collaboration of building envelope, building structure and building environmental system, the energy demand of this building is predicted to be less than 100 kWh/m² per year for heating, ventilation, cooling and artificial lighting.

completion	2001
client	Deutsche Post Bauen GmbH
area	73,501 square metres/791,200 square feet (tower gross floor area above ground)
structure	Concrete, steel
materials	Glass, steel
opposite	Southwest view at night
photography	Andreas Keller
top	Low building contains cafeteria, meeting and conference facilities
photography	Andreas Keller
bottom	Entrance
photography	HG Esch

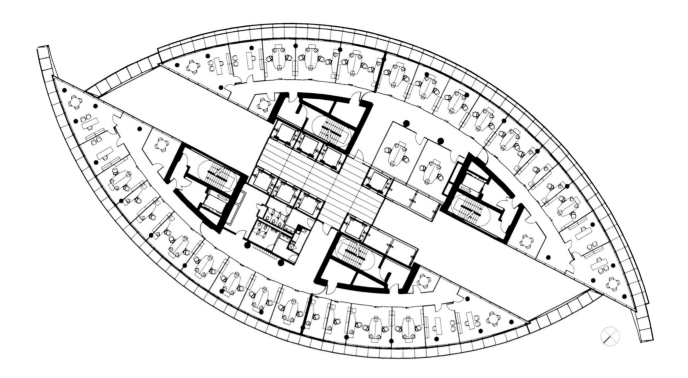

awards   Urban Land Institute 2001
                Best New Skyscrapers of the Year 2002
                AIA Chicago Chapter Award 2003
top   5th floor (typical floor)
above left   Skygarden
photography   Andreas Keller
above right   Lobby
photography   Atelier Altenkirch
opposite   Penthouse
photography   HG Esch

Springleaf Tower
Singapore
AC Martin Partners, Inc.

Springleaf Tower was built to house the
new headquarters of Southeast Asia's
largest real estate development firm.
It contains office spaces, an international
conferencing centre with advanced
telecommunications and electronic media
technology, adjacent gardens, executive
penthouse apartments, and parking for
200 cars.

Before embarking on the design stage, the
architects gained a valuable understanding
of the client's cultural, aesthetic, and
professional values and goals. Notably, the
Chinese philosophies of Feng Shui and
numerology informed some of the design
decisions.

The slender tower rises 37 storeys at the
corner of the site. A lantern-like crown acts
as a beacon when illuminated at night. The
rich textural appearance of the tower is
achieved by a stainless-steel skin that
covers the structural piers and is pierced by
a rhythmic pattern of window openings.
A sleek, seven-storey, glass-façade base, or
'podium', extends further along the block
and accommodates the public spaces of
the building – the main entrances, a grand
lobby, an international teleconferencing
centre with gardens, a lower-level link
to the subway stop, and an indoor
parking area.

At street level, a canopy supported by 60-
foot structural columns creates a covered
pedestrian promenade. The columns and
entranceways are highlighted by variegated,
salmon-coloured Brazilian granite, which,
together with the luminous steel skin and
glazing, as well as tropical landscaping,
allows the streetscape around the building
to blend into Singapore's 'garden city'
ambience.

Above the grand lobby, the tower floors are
filled with office spaces until the façade
steps in, forming the crown. Inside the
crown are two floors of private executive
penthouse apartments, capping the series
of luxurious amenities in Springleaf Tower.

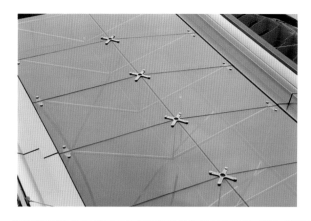

completion	2002
client	Ban Hin Leong Group (BHL)
area	37,160 square metres/400,000 square feet (37 storeys)
opposite	Springleaf harmonises with street and skyline
top	Detail and craft throughout the tower
bottom	Combination of round and rectangular forms
photography	Tim Griffith

opposite   Lobby glows like a lantern
top left   Windowed lobby open to the public
top right   Materials theme carries from exterior to interior
right   Dynamic glass welcomes guests
photography   Tim Griffith

Telenor World Headquarters
Fornebu, Oslo, Norway
Joint venture: NBBJ, HUS, PKA

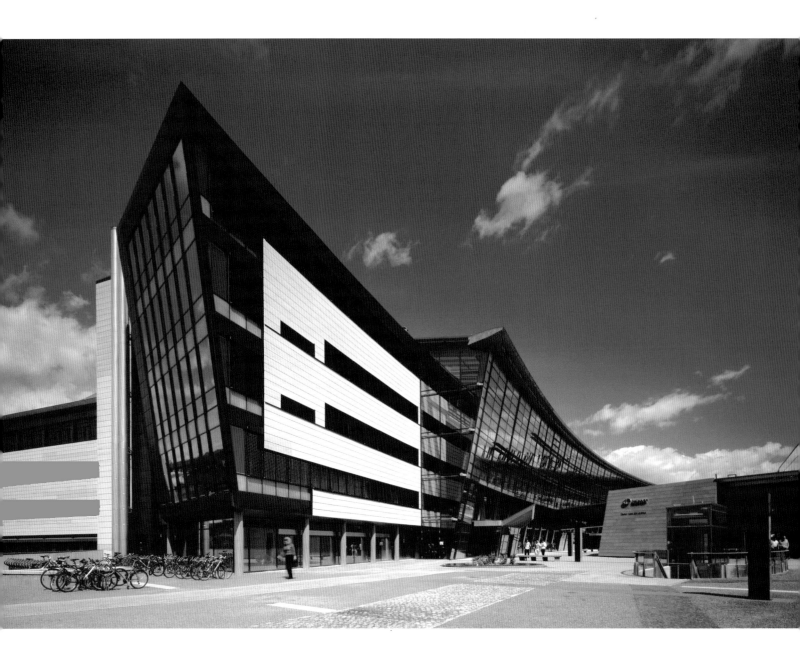

The new World Headquarters of Norway's telecommunications giant is a powerful expression of the company's vision to design the foremost creative working environment in Scandinavia. The idea to consolidate 7,700 employees at 6,000 workstations under eight roofs and atriums transforms the way in which Telenor conducts business, unifying the company, encouraging collaboration, and attracting the best employees in the industry.

The branching nature of the complex fosters increased communication, sensitivity to the environment, and employee well-being. Nestled unobtrusively into the open landscape of an old runway at the former Oslo International Airport, eight office wings branch out along the runway's east–west axis and are joined horizontally by two curved boulevards that embrace a central plaza.

A concept dubbed 'office of the future' brings the project's massive scale to a personal level. Offices are organised into working units of approximately 30 people, arranged individually or in modules of two or three units, configured to maximise workplace flexibility, natural lighting, and views of Oslofjord. An open floor plan, casual meeting places, and social amenities facilitate the exchange of ideas. Hot desks, laptop computers, and mobile devices provide utmost flexibility.

An aggressive 'green' agenda includes the use of water from the fjord as a heat exchanger, solar shading and natural ventilation combined with individual controls, and sustainable and non-toxic materials in the façade and interiors.

The Customer Centre, at the east end of the project, is a dramatic culmination of the building's movements with breathtaking views of Oslofjord and the city of Oslo. The new headquarters is both the cultural and commercial heart of the company. The workplace is not only functional, it is also meaningful. The building itself inspires employees to do their best, motivating the workforce to build performance for the company.

completion	September 2002
client	Telenor
area	158,000 square metres/1,700,000 square feet
cost	USD$342 million
structure	Prefabricated concrete, steel, glass curtainwall
opposite	View of main entrance featuring north boulevard, pedestrian bridge and learning centre
top	Aerial view of Telenor complex
bottom	Architect's sketch
photography	Tim Griffith

awards   National Honor Award, American Institute
         of Architects, 2003
         Best Technology Implementation, Bentley
         Systems, 1999

top   View of expo centre from southeast

left   View of north boulevard featuring entry
         canopy and expo centre

above   View of south boulevard and main plaza at
         dusk

photography   Tim Griffith

opposite top   Boulevard and atrium section B

opposite bottom   View of south boulevard entry canopy at
         dusk featuring pedestrian bridge

photography   Christian Richters

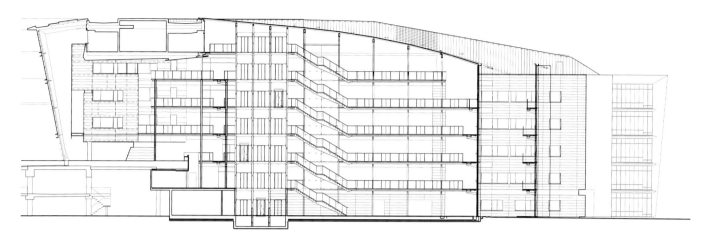

opposite top   Interior view of atrium in south boulevard, Building J

photography   Christian Richters

opposite bottom   View of plaza and north boulevard at night

photography   Tim Griffith

above   Interior view of north boulevard featuring view out to plaza

right   Interior view of atrium in south boulevard, Building J

photography   Christian Richters

Educational

70 **Carl and Ruth Shapiro Campus Center, Brandeis University**
Charles Rose Architects Inc

86 **Physics Institute, Humboldt University**
Augustin und Frank Architekten

58 **Admissions and Career Services Center, Trinity College**
Bohlin Cywinski Jackson

74 **Cranbrook Academy of Arts Addition**
Rafael Moneo

90 **School of Architecture, Florida International University**
Bernard Tschumi Architects

62 **Arenberg Library, Catholic University Of Leuven**
Rafael Moneo

78 **Lewis-Sigler Institute/Carl Icahn Laboratory, Princeton University**
Rafael Viñoly Architects

94 **The Australian Science and Mathematics School**
Woods Bagot

66 **Camino Nuevo Charter Academy Elementary School**
Daly Genik Architects

82 **Mediteknia, University of Kuopio**
Juhani Katainen Architects

96 **The Bahen Centre for Information Technology**
Diamond and Schmitt Architects Incorporated

Admissions and Career Services Center, Trinity College
Hartford, Connecticut, USA
Bohlin Cywinski Jackson

As the building that greets first-time visitors to the campus, the Admissions and Career Services Center must make a powerful impression. A primary design challenge was to site the building beside an important campus icon, the Chapel, and to preserve the quadrangle's grove of mature trees. The exterior configuration draws its forms, materials and scale from the adjacent residentially scaled buildings, as well as the Chapel. To help minimise its apparent mass, the Center is built into the slope so that only the top floor is visible from the primary approach through the Chapel quadrangle.

The top, entrance-level floor is a transparent pavilion housing the admissions office and sits on a solid base formed by the lower two floors. The building plan is organised around a north–south circulation spine. The spine is bisected by a central entry and lobby space, and is anchored by a monumental stairway and a great stone hearth.

The top floor is rendered as a glass and wood pavilion structured by a regular pattern of limestone piers. The rhythm established by the limestone piers and their detailing resonates with the Chapel's Gothic buttresses, and forms a cloister-like edge for the Chapel quadrangle, while providing transparency and views to the rest of the campus.

The roof is green slate, to complement the Chapel's roof. The entrance side of the top-floor pavilion is softened by vine-covered trellises. The lower two floors relate to the original buildings on the Long Walk in their rusticated brownstone cladding and more opaque faces punctuated by discrete window openings and slender limestone fins. The interior spaces all carefully reveal views of the campus and evoke the spirit of the institution. Anchored around a massive brownstone fireplace, the Admissions and Career Services Center has the ambience of a comfortable living room.

completion	September 2001
client	Trinity College
area	2880 square metres/31,000 square feet
structure	Structural steel frame, glue-laminated heavy timber
materials	Brownstone, Indiana limestone, green slate roof, bluestone flooring, cherry veneer casework
cost	USD$11.5 million
opposite	East elevation view from soccer fields
top	South elevation; view to large meeting room
bottom	Interior view of large meeting room looking south
photography	Karl Backus

awards   AIA Philadelphia Honor Award for Design
         Excellence 2001
         Chicago Athenaeum American Architecture
         Award 2002
         AIA Pennsylvania Merit for Excellence in
         Architectural Design 2002
         AIA Connecticut Design Award 2002

top   South terrace showing memorial fountain
         and limestone and timber trellis

right   Interior lobby showing timber/steel trusses
         and great brownstone hearth

photographer   Mike Thomas

opposite top   Section

opposite bottom   Great brownstone fireplace in lobby

photography   Karl Backus

60 Educational Admissions and Career Services Center, Trinity College

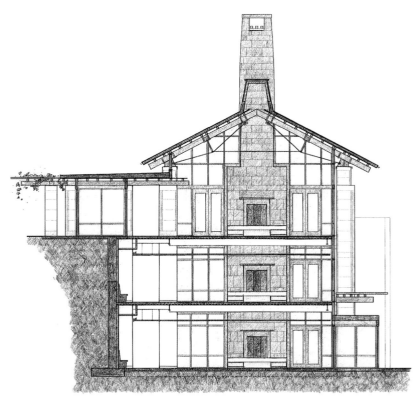

Arenberg Library, Catholic University of Leuven
Leuven, Belgium
Rafael Moneo

The Arenberg Campus library envelops the remains of a Celestine monastery, built in 1526, keeping an important historic site alive while integrating it into the life of the city and of the University.

The architects' aim from the outset was to maintain the scale and the character of the site and to make the tiny cloister the core of the new library. The design strategy relied on erecting a building that would enclose the cloister. The construction of this building provided a new and unexpected space, a new courtyard, flanked by the remains of the friars' rooms and by the walls of the old surrounding buildings of the Monastery. This newly found courtyard has become a counterpoint to the enclosed cloister. The organic geometry of the new construction invigorates and animates the severe cloister while also making a gesture of welcome in the access court reached either from the path on the hillside or from the road.

The intense use of the ground and the desire to keep the building as low as possible led the architects to place the compact book deposit in the basement of the new building. The open stacks are located in the basement and ground floor levels, extending in horizontal planes between the existing brick walls facing the road and the reading room in the former refectory attached to the cloister.

The lower level of the open stacks receives light from skylights placed above the reading areas on the floor above while a series of triangular skylights brings natural light to the open stacks on the ground floor. As a result, the existing volumes maintain their value and the rooftop of the old refectory continues to be the most striking element.

completed	2002
client	Catholic University of Leuven
area	10,616 square metres/114,300 square feet
opposite	Cloister
below	Skylights in the roof over book stacks
bottom	Entrance
photography	Duccio Malagamba

above, below and opposite   Views of library reading rooms
photography   Duccio Malagamba

Camino Nuevo Charter Academy Elementary School
Los Angeles, California, USA
Daly Genik Architects

This elementary school is the first of several projects Daly Genik is designing for the Camino Nuevo Charter Academy. A non-profit community support group in Westlake founded this charter school campus, comprising an elementary school for 250 children, a middle school for 250, and a shared playground. Created in response to crisis conditions and over-crowding in the local schools, this charter school campus is a haven for elementary school children in the Westlake/MacArthur Park area of Los Angeles.

The first phase of the project, the new elementary school, is conceived as two parts: the existing mini-mall on the site, which retains its L-shaped form, and an addition that creates a new entry and face to the street. Reusing and renovating a former mini-mall and parking lots have transformed this familiar type of low-slung building into an inviting 12-classroom elementary school around a courtyard. The three main elements include a new freestanding extension which widens the upstairs passageways, allowing ambient light into the classrooms; the sloping parking lot, which is converted into a pleasant outdoor assembly/play area; and curved wooden lattices that shade most of the building.

Due to the constrained site, all spaces (indoor and outdoor) are maximised to provide efficient and flexible learning spaces. An intense planning effort by the architects resulted in the congregation of complementary activity spaces. The goal of creating the charter school was to form a building that was inviting and invigorating to the local community.

completed	September 2000
client	Pueblo Nuevo Development
area	1860 square metres/20,000 square feet
materials	Stucco, concrete, Nexwood
cost	USD$1.7 million
awards	Rudy Bruner Award for Urban Excellence, Gold Medal 2003; Westside Urban Forum Award; AIA/Los Angeles Design Award
opposite	View of main courtyard during recess
top	View of front entry
bottom	Stair detail
photography	Tom Bonner

top	Overview of building on Burlington Street
right	Benches line the upper floor screen
photography	Tom Bonner
opposite top	Photograph of the mini-mall prior to design and construction.
photography	Daly Genik
opposite middle	View of enclosed courtyard, now used for a play space and outdoor cafeteria
photography	Tom Bonner
opposite bottom	Axometric of screen addition

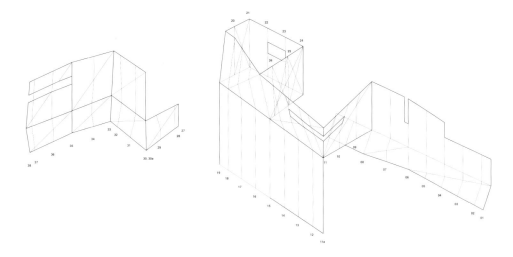

Carl and Ruth Shapiro Campus Center, Brandeis University
Waltham, Massachusetts, USA
Charles Rose Architects Inc

The new 6040-square-metre campus centre at Brandeis University contributes significantly to the modern architecture of the University as well as the architecture of the Boston area. Brandeis, which was founded in 1948, offered no obvious site for the campus centre. Charles Rose Architects tackled this problem by placing it at the geographical heart of the campus, a nod to the centre's goal of heightening the quality of student life and a symbolic gesture that puts the student at the centre of the university. A parking lot and aging building were demolished to make way for the centre, which opened the way for new lines of access that link it to the admissions and administrative buildings, the Rose Art Museum and a large theatre. Significantly, the centre creates new landscapes, including a courtyard, gardens and an expansive central green space that the Post-War campus did not have before. The centre itself is really two buildings, connected by a three-storey atrium. By creating two separate wings, the architects not only create distinctive parts for the building's many functions but also offer a gracious means for the majority of rooms to enjoy tremendous amounts of natural light – a real plus for the monotonous New England winter. The atrium is criss-crossed by catwalks that connect the building's upper levels. Intensely sculptural in design, the exterior of the north side is clad in pre-patinated copper panels, which enhance the building's sculptural volume; limestone and copper clad the south side, which is also marked by a coloured-glass curtain wall. Completed in October 2002, the campus centre is the new home to a 350-seat theatre, computer library, recital hall, student clubs, bookstore and café.

completion	October, 2002
client	Brandeis University
area	6040 square metres/65,000 square feet
materials	Limestone, pre-patinated copper, glass, Terrazzo, oak paneling, stainless steel rails, aluminium windows
opposite	View from southeast
top	View from east; south volume is separated from north volume by atrium
bottom	Detail at east; 3-storey glass wall permits dramatic views of campus
photography	Chuck Choi Architectural Photography

right	First floor plan
bottom	Detail of west façade
opposite left	Detail view of atrium staircase looking north
opposite right	View of library reading room
opposite bottom	Section at atrium
photography	Chuck Choi Architectural Photography

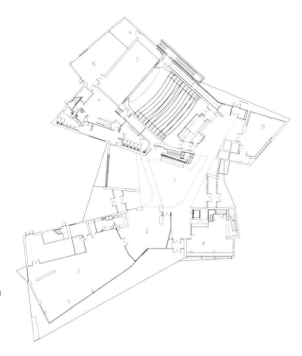

1 Atrium
2 Café
3 Bookstore
4 IT library
5 Theatre
6 Backstage
7 Greenroom
8 Lounge
9 Fellowes garden
10 Classroom building
11 Faculty centre
12 Administration building

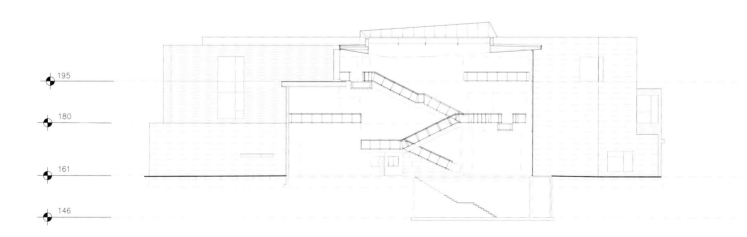

195

180

161

146

Cranbrook Academy of Arts Addition
Bloomfield Hills, Michigan, USA
Rafael Moneo

Cranbrook, founded in 1904, was at first a primary and boarding school with an emphasis placed on the connection between education and nature. As its curriculum extended to include applied and fine arts, a number of famous designers were involved in the evolving campus, leading to its reputation as one of the most important schools of art and applied art in the USA.

The project is part of an initiative by the Cranbrook Educational Community to complete and improve the campus installations. New installations were created for three departments: ceramics, art and textile and metalworking.

The first concern of the designers was to determine what kind of building could coexist next to the resonant volume of the existing Eliel Saarinen-designed museum. The architects intended to integrate the back of the museum into the new building while at the same time maintaining complete visual autonomy from the existing iconic fountain, the Rape of Europa.

Two observations can be made about the floor plan. One is the importance of the transition piece in the ground floor as well as in the upper floor where galleries for exhibiting student work are to be installed with the intention that their work will be seen in conjunction with the pieces presented in the museum. The other is that the work spaces for the students and the studio for the artist-in-residence use the same equipment for the development of their work, emphasising the closeness between students and faculty that has always been characteristic of the Academy. Regarding the character of the building, an attempt has been made to maintain the industrial aspect of the studios designed by Saarinen, while not altering either the scale or the materials used. Special attention was also paid to the landscaping.

completion	2002
client	Cranbrook Educational Community
area	3275 square metres/35,250 square feet
cost	USD$8,145,000 (budget)
opposite	View of studio wing
top	Exhibition gallery
bottom	Workshop wing
photography	Duccio Malagamba

top   Existing museum by Eliel Saarinen with
          entrance to new studio addition
left   Exhibition gallery
right   New stair hall with student exhibit space
photography   Duccio Malagamba

Lewis-Sigler Institute/Carl Icahn Laboratory, Princeton University
Princeton, New Jersey USA
Rafael Viñoly Architects

The unique mission of the Lewis-Sigler Institute for Integrative Genomics at Princeton University is to conduct pioneering research into fundamental questions of biology by integrating the perspectives and analytical tools of molecular biology, chemistry, physics and computer analysis. To help achieve the goals of the Institute, the Carl Icahn Laboratory, among the first fully integrated labs in America, was designed to unite researchers from a variety of disciplines and to encourage a free exchange of thoughts and findings.

Situated between the science complex of brick-clad buildings within the historical campus of traditional stone, the building bridges both contexts with its skin of precast concrete panels which have the proportion and colour of brick and a texture that mimics the richness of stone. In plan, it is composed of a curved glass façade positioned on the south edge of the site, and two rectangular building blocks on the north and east edges, which contain the laboratories. Beyond the specific program needs of individual labs, the building design was determined by the paramount need for flexibility over time as research and researchers change with the pace of genomic science.

The space between the lab volumes and the curved boundary of the 'quad' is spanned by a steel truss roof that shelters an open communal area known as the Atrium. This space is enclosed by a glass curtain wall with vertical louvres that track the movement of the sun in the southern sky. Their synchronised rotation throughout the day keeps them at the optimal angle for shading the interior of the institute, while also limiting the thermal loading on the building's cooling systems.

The functional arrangement, flexible spaces, ample provision of natural light and distinctive safety features that this building incorporates promote the vigorous initiatives of the Institute and inspire scientific inquiry.

completion	January 2003
client	Princeton University
area	12,820 square metres/138,000 square feet
structure	Precast concrete shell and frameless glass curtain wall with vertical cable system
materials	Exterior louvre system made from extruded aluminium slats, hydraulically driven; interior materials include epoxy terrazzo, clear maple, fabric panel, painted steel
cost	USD$48.4 million
opposite	View from circular playing field
top	Exterior view of cantilevered conference room at southeast entry
right	View to northeast entrance at Washington Road
photography	Román Viñoly

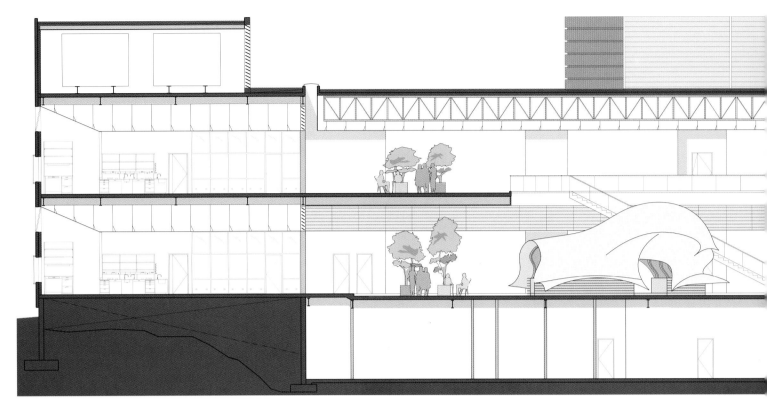

awards   New York Council Society of American
           Registered Architects, Eighth Annual Design
           Awards Program Award of Excellence, 2003
           American Institute of Architects, New York
           State Award of Excellence 2003
           Contract Magazine 25th Annual Interiors
           Awards Competition, Educational Facilities
           Category 2003
           American Institute of Architects New Jersey,
           Design Award for Excellence,
           Silver Award 2003
above   East section
below left View of interior auditorium
below right Second floor plan
opposite   Interior atrium seating area
photography Román Viñoly

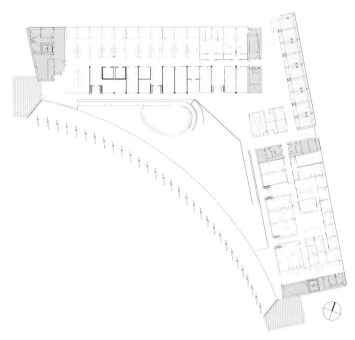

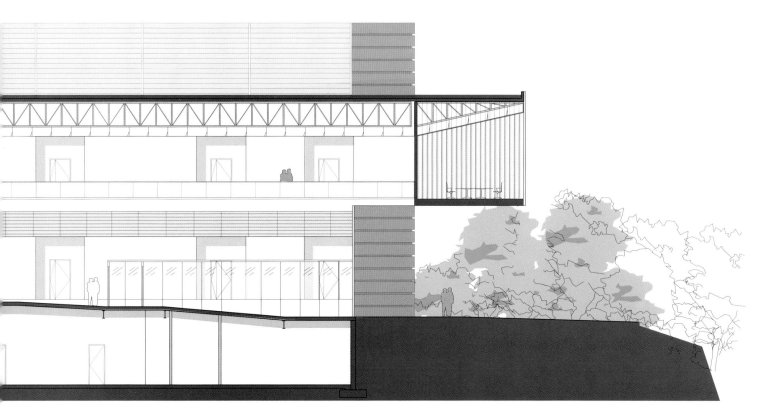

Mediteknia, University of Kuopio

Kuopio, Finland
Juhani Katainen Architects

Mediteknia is a new, independent addition to an existing university building that was built as a result of an architectural competition held in the 1970s. It is a multidisciplinary institute of applied science that brings together clinical research, drug research, food and health research and a learning centre, with a clinical trial centre at its core. Mediteknia is expected to increase collaboration between the university drug research groups and the pharmaceutical industry.

The architectural concept of the building is partly a factor of the existing buildings and the sloping site, but some new techniques have been incorporated into the construction. The building comprises offices, study rooms, laboratories, research rooms, a cafeteria and an auditorium.

completion	2003
client	Senaatti-kiinteistöt Oy
area	8170 square metres/87,940 square feet
structure	Post and beam construction, concrete slabs and columns, steel beams
materials	Red brick, metal sheeting, steel, glass
opposite	Upper courtyard, glassed steel structure protects stairs from heavy snow during winter
bottom left	Entrance area
bottom right	Cafeteria
photography	Hannu Koivisto, Juhani Katainen Architects

below   Auditorium lobby, cafeteria to left,
                 cloakrooms to right
opposite top   Auditorium
opposite bottom   Roof-lit lobby viewed from first floor
photography   Hannu Koivisto, Juhani Katainen Architects

Physics Institute, Humboldt University

Berlin, Germany
Augustin und Frank Architekten

The Humboldt University Physics Institute is part of the Adlershof scientific research site in the southeastern suburbs of Berlin. A masterplan has been developed for the area, which is currently dominated by the plastic building shells of the aerodynamic experimental buildings of the 1930s.

The Physics Institute building is, while integrated into the plan as a whole, a solitary structure with four independent outer skins. The internal structure is visible from the exterior, giving the building a sense of transparency and openness. Internal garden courtyards separate the different zones of the Institute, which is organised around the principle of rooms radiating from a central core. This results in easy orientation, short distances and flexibility in the use of the space.

With the exception of the north façade, every outer part of the building incorporates easy-maintenance walkways equipped with different shading devices. All hallways have vegetative sun protection through overgrown steel and bamboo trellis, which are mounted along the walkway of the façade. Every lounge area has an outside shading device. The outside walls are carried as light constructions over the supporting structure of reinforced concrete. The building concept focuses on enhancing and influencing the development at Adlershof. The area will continually evolve, unlike the formulated city town-planning model. Because of this, the concept is that of an 'evolvable' building.

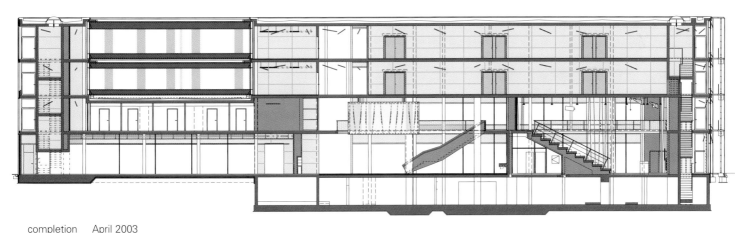

completion	April 2003
client	City of Berlin
area	20,500 square metres/220,700 square feet (gross area)
materials	Coloured concrete, industrial glazing (glass panels), steel, aluminium, concrete
cost	EUR50 million
awards	Distinction, Architectural Award Berlin 2003
opposite	Northwest view at night, showing light patterns
top	Southeast view, walkway and installation for ranking plants
middle	East side of building
bottom	Cross section
photography	Werner Huthmacher

opposite top   Courtyard, view through the two-storey courtyard opening and 'bridge' to surrounding landscape

opposite bottom   Lecture theatre for experimental physics

left   Courtyard, detail of façade area, walkway and vegetative sun protection

bottom   Entrance hall with hovering, glowing conference area (seminar room) and staircase to main entrance of lecture hall

photography   Werner Huthmacher

School of Architecture, Florida International University
Miami, Florida, USA
Bernard Tschumi Architects

The School of Architecture at F.I.U. has been described as a 'commuter' school, where students divide their time between an office where they earn a living, the School where they study, and the home where they often oversee family responsibilities. Often considered an impediment, this situation can be turned into an advantage. This project argues that computer technology has freed designers from the fixity of the drafting table – disks and files can be emailed instantly anywhere, and the location of actual work becomes secondary. What is primary, however, is the social exchange, the discussion, debate, and clash of ideas between friends, colleagues, and teachers. This can happen only at the School. Between computers and social interaction, the School at F.I.U. introduces a new type of strategy, suggesting a new educational model.

The architect describes the project as the sobriety of two wings defining a space activated by the exuberance of two colourful 'generators'. The wings are made of white precast concrete and the two generators of varied yellow and red ceramic tiles.

The new buildings are arranged around an event-oriented central courtyard (60 x 90 feet) with the vibrant 'generators'; containing a lecture hall, reading room and gallery, and the minimalist white wings housing the studio and offices. Gathering together all of the school circulation and major social and cultural spaces, the central generators shade the courtyard during the morning and late afternoon hours. Whatever the level of attendance on any given day, one can observe the constant activity of students on the covered walkways, shaded steps, roof terraces, and in the courtyard and studio.

completion	March 2003
client	Florida International University
area	9500 square metres/102,000 square feet
materials	Concrete, ceramic tiles, glass, metal handrails
cost	USD$130 per square foot
opposite	View of gallery/reading room (centre) studio wing (left)
top	Architect's sketch
middle	Street view of studio
bottom	Street view of lecture hall
photography	Peter Mauss/Esto

top   Corner view of gallery/reading room
middle   View towards courtyard
right   Corner view of gallery/reading room
opposite top left   View towards courtyard from elevated
                walkway
opposite top right Interior – office wing
opposite   Courtyard stair
photography   Peter Mauss/Esto

The Australian Science and Mathematics School

Flinders University, Adelaide, South Australia, Australia
Woods Bagot

The Australian Science and Mathematics School (ASMS) is a comprehensive senior secondary school, which acts as a catalyst for advances in teacher preparation and professional development through education, business and industry partnerships, using new and emerging technologies and enterprise initiatives. A key feature of the school is the replacement of classrooms and laboratories with 'learning commons' and 'learning studios'.

'Home-base' work stations exist within learning commons, providing personal desk and storage stations for 50 students. The learning studios contain specialist services and hands-on facilities, enabling students to undertake practical work and experiments that support activities in the learning commons. Operable walls or partial partitions between learning commons allow flexibility.

The heart of the school, the central common, promotes a sense of community within the school and provides a strong visual identity with an impressive two-storey space providing outlook and access to the bushland gully and outdoor spaces. It was considered important that the building design incorporate best practice in environmentally sustainable design and intelligent building concepts. To meet this objective the school incorporates a 'mixed mode' air conditioning system which can operate with a full fresh air economy cycle or solely by natural ventilation through a low and high level louvre system in the façade and central roof lights.

Intelligent building controls also respond to climatic conditions and occupants' requirements to optimise comfort conditions and minimise energy use. The building itself has become a learning tool for the school, enabling students to develop an understanding of how buildings, people and the natural environment interact. The output from the building control system is linked to the school intranet, providing information on the performance of the building's active and passive systems.

completion	March 2003
client	Department of Education & Children's Services (DECS), South Australian Government
area	Approximately 4,000 square metres/43,060 square feet
structure	Suspended slabs, concrete columns, steel roof framing, precast or metal deck cladding to east and west, glazed cladding to north and south
cost	AUD$14 million
awards	Designshare Awards 2003 Merit Award Royal Australian Institute of Architects South Australian Chapter Awards 2003, Commendation

opposite top	Northern façade with sun control louvres
opposite bottom	Entry defined by double-height window wall and cantilevered roof plain
top	Community assembly space eastern window wall
bottom	Community assembly space interior
photography	Kevin O'Daley, Aspect Photography

The Bahen Centre for Information Technology, University of Toronto

Toronto, Ontario, Canada
Diamond and Schmitt Architects Incorporated

The Bahen Centre for Information Technology at the University of Toronto accommodates teaching and research in computer science, electrical engineering, engineering science, mechanical and industrial engineering.

The building achieves a high level of flexibility in program, configuration and servicing with the concept of a high-tech loft space. All power, data communication, heating, ventilation and air conditioning is delivered through an accessible floor with concrete tiles. Ceilings are formed by coffered cast-concrete vaults which accommodate direct and indirect lighting and acoustic absorption to dampen room noise. A three-storey skylar arcade bisects the mid-block site and provides access to all lecture and seminar rooms. A circular public stair surrounds a tower of shared meeting rooms that links all eight levels. The glass cylinder is skylit and draws daylight deep into the building.

At the seventh and eighth floors an exterior courtyard faces west and provides a welcome terrace in the midst of the research centres.

To the south, a new landscaped quadrangle is enclosed by existing buildings to the east, south and west and is overlooked by a two-storey interior court and café.

An existing driveway, between the Fields Institute and the Koffler Centre for Student Services, was transformed into a pedestrian walk, lined with trees and bordered by a rivulet of water flowing from the quadrangle pool, in a balustrade at waist height.

Along St. George Street, the built form steps down to three stories in height to match the cornice of the Koffler Centre. This wing enveloped a designated historic Victorian house in a small courtyard opening off the street. The retention of this house was mandated. Rather than stop the building south of the house, a pavilion emulating the proportional system of the house was extended to the north with a translucent glass link forming a backdrop to the Victorian building.

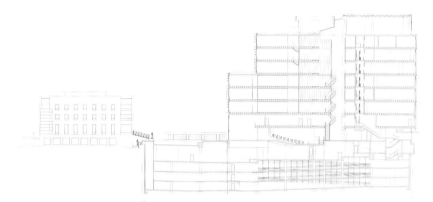

completion	April 2002
client	University of Toronto, Faculty of Applied Science and Engineering, Faculty of Arts and Science
area	37,000 square metres/398,300 square feet (above grade); 10,500 square metres/ 113,000 square feet (below grade)
materials	Sand coloured precast concrete, Norman white clay bricks, masonry-recycled kaolin clay, aluminium and frit glass sunshades
cost	CAD$102 million
opposite	Atrium with café and sun shade covered windows
top	Section
bottom	Front elevation at night
photography	Steven Evans

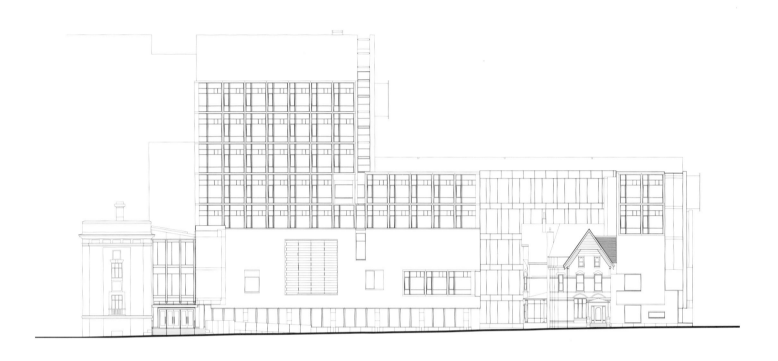

awards   Architecture and Urban Design Award,
Award of Excellence 2003
Ontario Association of Architects,
Architectural Excellence Award 2003
Ontario Concrete Awards, Architectural
Merit, Precast and Cast-in-place
Concrete 2003
Illuminating Engineering Society,
Sectional and Regional Illumination
Design Award 2003
Canadian Architect magazine 2001
Art of Cadd Award 2001

opposite middle   East elevation
opposite bottom left   Fountain in south courtyard
opposite bottom right   South courtyard from College Street
top right   Meeting rooms and skylight drum at top
of stair atrium
middle left   Study area
bottom left   View from second floor looking east
towards stair
bottom right   View through stair and screen to slot
atrium
photography   Steven Evans

Institutional

114 Max Planck Institute of
Molecular Cell Biology and
Genetics
Heikkinen-Komonen Architects

102 ABS House
Woods Bagot

118 Media Authority Building
Koen van Velsen

106 French Embassy
Christian de Portzamparc

122 The Embassy of Finland
Gullichsen Vormala Architects

110 Madrid Regional Documentary
Centre
Mansilla + Tuñón Architects

126 Umoja House, Co-location
Embassy Building
The Manser Practice

ABS House
Belconnen, Australian Capital Territory, Australia
Woods Bagot

The client's brief called for a building that represented its mission and core values. The Australian Bureau of Statistics (ABS) is a prominent federal government organisation that has been central to the growth and well-being of the Belconnen Town Centre for many years. As a founding member of the Town Centre and a major source of employment, it was important to create a building with a strong civic presence in the heart of Belconnen. Central to the design concept was the need to integrate the ABS organisation in a building that fosters a sense of community within the various divisions of the Australian Bureau of Statistics. A central atrium creates a vertical 'village common', fostering visual interaction between the larger community and building users. The atrium forms an 'internal street', providing a continuous public realm within and through the building. The sky-bridges that cross the atrium at upper levels provide informal break-out spaces for casual interactive exchanges within the workplace, supporting the new culture of the ABS. The design of the external spaces similarly addresses organisational requirements as well as responding to environmental and urban design factors. A private courtyard is located to the north of the building to optimise solar penetration. It is accessible from the public level within the building yet secure access is maintained. This space is also cut into the existing site contours to isolate it from acoustic and visual interference of the adjacent bus station. The integration of environmentally sustainable design principles was fundamental to the design approach. Woods Bagot and the client were committed to creating an energy efficient building. The building utilises passive and active environmental systems that provide opportunities to maximise natural light and fresh air for workplace and break-out areas.

completion   March 2002
client   The Australian Bureau of Statistics
area   41,259 square metres/444,100 square feet
structure   Precast concrete panels, aluminium composite panels, custom expressed fixings, aluminium sandwich panel, insitu concrete and painted CFC sheeting, Colorbond Kliplok metal sheeting, two-sided silicone curtain wall suite
opposite   Prominent southwest corner is locked to ground by a folded roof element
top   Atrium is visually connected to streetscape
bottom   Public through-site link mediates the change in level across site
photography   Eric Sierins

top   Re-centring blade wall accommodates
             reception and level 1 break-out areas
above   Ground floor reception is incorporated into
             a blade wall that also supports central
             staircase
above right   Central 'Village Common' looking west
opposite   Central atrium looking east from main entry
photography Eric Sierins

The Australian Bureau of Statistics exists and encourages informed decision making, research and discussion within governments and the community by providing a high quality, objective and responsive national statistical service

French Embassy

Berlin, Germany
Christian de Portzamparc architect
Elizabeth de Portzamparc interior architecture and furniture

The French Embassy in Germany is built on one of Berlin's most beautiful squares, the Pariser Platz. The building has a massive façade of cement and stone with openings designed to relate to those in the nearby Brandenburg Gate, responding to the restrictions imposed by its historical setting. The cramped, L-shaped site is bordered by two large, long blind walls and the crucial question was how to integrate the numerous services of the Embassy in such a confined space. De Portzamparc worked around the theme of openings, proposing a stone basement, a noble level with larger windows and an attic level with a roof garden.

The architect's wish was that no office would be without natural light. The closed urban block was opened up by creating a 6-metre internal street, linking the Pariser Platz on one end and the Wilhelmstrasse at the other. This covered walkway, from which one can see not only the sky, but also out at both ends and an inner courtyard at ground level, organises the accesses and makes it easy to comprehend the block as a whole. It also features a large garden on natural soil on the first level and a birch-lined promenade over 100 metres long on the fourth level.

In addition to housing the embassy's administrative areas, the building also aims to represent and promote French culture in Germany, with an exhibition space, an auditorium for conferences and shows and a library. The interior architecture, and the furniture of the noble level and the residence were designed by Elizabeth de Portzamparc, achieving a spirit of architectural coherence.

completion	January 2003
area	18,000 square metres/193,800 square feet
cost	EUR38 million
opposite top	View towards cafeteria from garden at night
photography	Gitty Darugar
opposite bottom	Main façade on the Pariser Platz, incorporates balance of horizontal and vertical rhythms
top	Raised garden on natural soil inside the closed and narrow site
bottom	Meeting rooms building at night
photography	Nicholas Borel

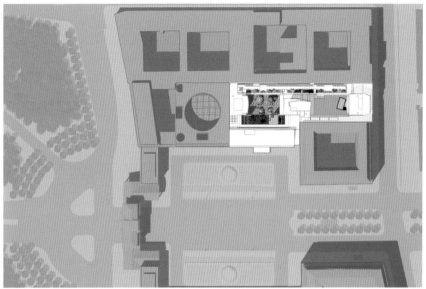

opposite   Garden on natural soil on the first level,
            behind the meeting rooms building
top   Site plan
above   Elizabeth de Portzamparc's original project
            for the reception hall. Carpet and painting
            by François Rouan.
photography Nicholas Borel

Madrid Regional Documentary Centre

Madrid, Spain

Mansilla + Tuñón Architects

The Madrid Regional Government Archives and Library in the former El Águila brewery is a centre for the preservation, custody and dissemination of the Region's historic documentary heritage, and is ultimately aimed at ensuring the transparency of administrative processes and citizen's rights. The project is a result of a 1994 public competition. The unusual site, a former brewery with large, open spaces, was the catalyst and inspiration for the winning design by Mansilla + Tuñón Architects.

The Regional Archives buildings cover 30,000 square metres (322,900 square feet), and are organised into three modules: contributions, storage and public access. The storage building can hold 100 kilometres (62 miles) of shelving, structured into six equal floors, surrounded by a thermal quilt in the form of a translucent double façade; the ground plan organisation is a response to the challenge of producing architecture within the limits imposed by the strict fire prevention regulations.

The Regional Library covers 10,000 square metres (107,600 square feet). It responds to the need for a diverse multimedia library programme through the renovation of the former industrial spaces. The silos that once held barley now hold every book published in the Madrid region.

For Madrid, the integrated Regional Archives and Library complex is like two intertwined hands, a symbol of the convergence between environment and architecture. One hand shelters and protects the historic heritage and the other provides protection for the local culture, our future heritage.

completion	2002
client	Madrid Regional Government
area	40,000 square metres/430,600 square feet
materials	Concrete structure, u-glass, zinc roofing, aluminium shingles
awards	Premio del Colegio de Arquitectos de Madrid 2003
opposite	General view
top	Library
middle	Exterior view
bottom	Archive building
photography	Luis Asín

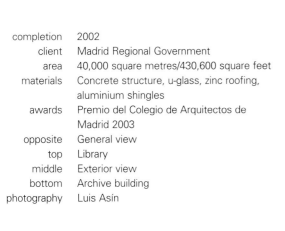

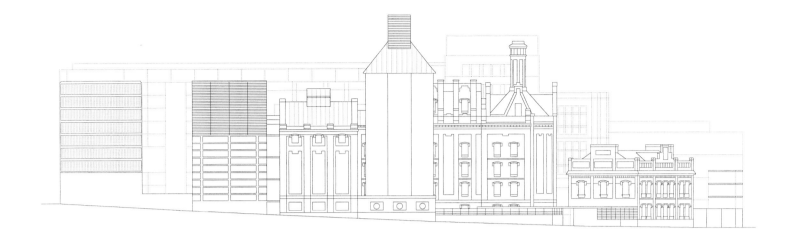

top   East elevation
right   Regional Archive
opposite top Section
opposite left Interior street
opposite right Main lobby of library
photography Luis Asín

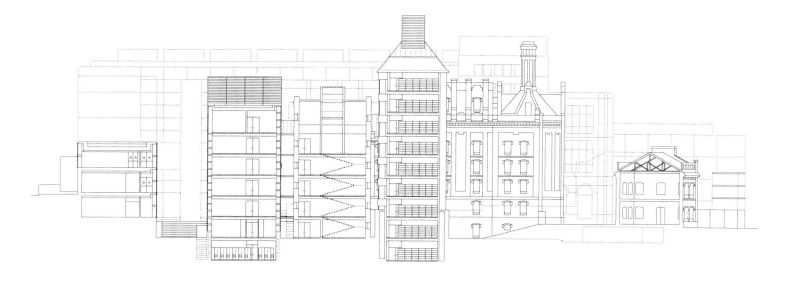

Max Planck Institute of Molecular Cell Biology and Genetics
Dresden, Germany
Heikkinen-Komonen Architects

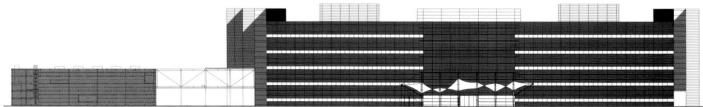

Located on the banks of the river Elbe, the molecular biological research centre consists of three buildings. The laboratory block is the largest and contains six autonomous research units sharing common service and administrative areas, a library, café, restaurant and 300-seat auditorium. The units are grouped around the full-height reception foyer where scientists can meet each other while lunching, reading professional journals, negotiating, or having a coffee break. A roof-top pergola provides another opportunity for informal interaction. The laboratory building is clad externally in deep blue aluminium. A veil of oxidised copper mesh on the front of the façade provides interest while protecting the internal working areas from the sun. The effect of the green aluminium grille on the deep blue wall varies according to the viewer's movement and position.

The animal breeding and hatchery building is a windowless building containing various controlled environments for animals, fly breeding and hatcheries. The third building contains residential apartments for visiting research workers, as well as additional offices. It is divided into two sections by a Japanese garden.

completion	2001
client	Max-Planck-Gesellschaft zur Förderung der Wissenschaften
area	22,070 square metres/237,600 square feet
opposite top	Laboratory façades are shaded by a green aluminium grille
opposite bottom	Elevation
top	Concrete element façades of animal research building are covered with galvanised metal mesh
bottom	View from street
photography	Jussi Tiainen

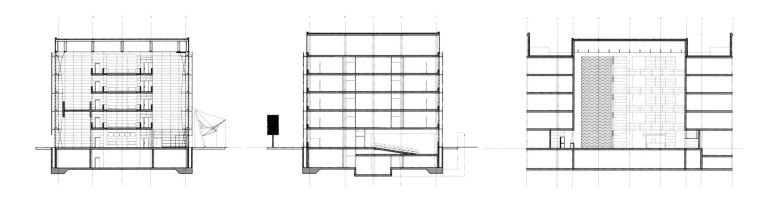

opposite top	Main entrance and sail canopy
opposite left	Maintenance yard between animal research building and laboratory can be closed off with sliding galvanised metal walls
opposite right	Part of George Steinmann's 'Metalog' artwork
top	Sections
above left	Restaurant
above right	Lounge space on mezzanine level of central hall
photography	Jussi Tiainen

Media Authority Building

Hilversum, The Netherlands
Koen van Velsen

The Dutch Media Authority, (Commissariaat voor de Media) is an independent body that monitors national broadcasting corporations and administers the Dutch Media Act. The new office of the Media Authority is located close to the Hilversum 'Media Park', home of a variety of other media-related businesses. The architect's aim was to create a relationship between the building, its users, and the surrounding wooded setting. Tranquility and well-being are the main themes of the design. The building nestles into the sloping site (the entrance level is 2 metres below the rear façade), with existing and new trees projecting through cut-out sections of a cantilevered roof at the main entrance, further adding to the incorporation of nature into the architecture. Similarly, internal courtyards have been cut out of the building volume around several pre-existing trees, increasing daylight deep into the building. The building's corridors, which gradually assimilate the increasing difference in floor level, are located along the two long façades. The offices are reached via secondary passageways at right angles to the façade. As people walk along the corridors, openings and large areas of glass in the façade afford glimpses of the surrounding landscape. The work areas, by contrast, have views onto the internal courtyards. Unlike the external façades of glass and metal, the courtyard façades present staggered windows, masonry walls and vivid splashes of colour.

completion	2001
client	Media Authority, Hilversum
area	2048 square metres/22,040 square feet (floor area)
cost	EUR3.4 million
opposite	Trees project through cantilevered entrance canopy
right	Internal courtyards bring colour and nature to surrounding offices
photography	Duccio Malagamba

opposite top   Large windows blur distinction between inside and outside
opposite bottom   Main entrance
top   Internal corridor
bottom   Entrance hall has inside/outside feel
photography   Duccio Malagamba

The Embassy of Finland
Stockholm, Sweden,
Gullichsen Vormala Architects

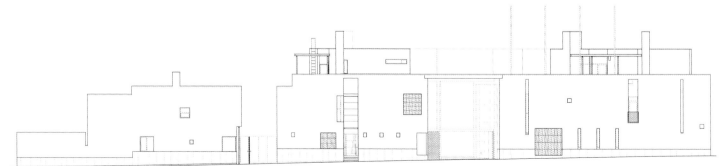

The Embassy building is located in the diplomatic quarter of Djurgården. The triangular site accommodates the Embassy and consulate offices, a banqueting hall, a separate staff residence wing and sauna facilities. The ambassador's official residence is located outside the Embassy complex.

The principal architectural feature of the building is the long wall of the street façade. A tall gate in the wall opens to a palazzo-like paved courtyard, around which the offices of the Embassy are organised. The residential wing has a separate access through its own courtyard. The two dwellings open into a private garden.

The Embassy takes advantage of the spectacular position on the south side of the historic Gärdet field. The official suite opens through a main garden to this open meadow. During the summer months, the garden acts as an extension of the banquet hall. The ambassador's office on the second floor of the chancellory overlooks the garden and the undulating landscape.

The Finnish Embassy in Sweden attempts to communicate on the level of the collective memory of the two nations with their 600 years of shared history. For that reason, the perspective of the architectural language has been expanded along the time axis to a greater magnitude than usual.

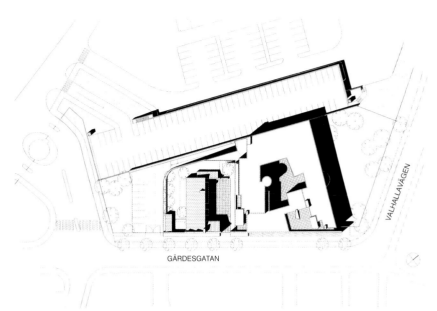

VALHALLAVÄGEN

GÄRDESGATAN

completion	2002
client	Ministry for Foreign Affairs, Finland
area	4520 square metres/48,650 square feet
cost	USD$13.3 million
opposite top	View from Gärdesgatan
opposite bottom	Gärdesgatan elevation
top	Site plan
bottom	View from courtyard (Borggård)
photography	Jussi Tiainen

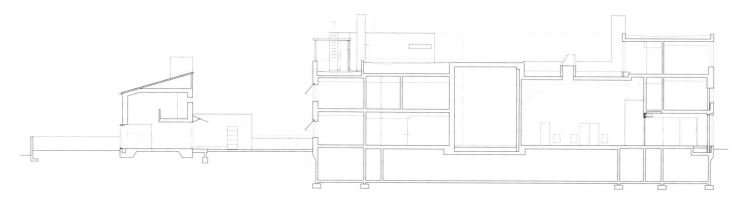

top Section B
bottom View from garden
photography Jussi Tiainen
opposite View from library
opposite top View from terrace
photography Camilla Wirseen
opposite bottom View from foyer
photography Jussi Tiainen

Umoja House, Co-location Embassy Building
Dar es Salaam, Tanzania
The Manser Practice

The design was developed from the diverse requirements of five government organisations based in Europe and their missions in Tanzania. Security issues, demands of the climate, and the technical and practical constraints resulting from the local economy and conditions were other major factors that had to be incorporated into the design.

The building consists of two blocks of office accommodation, which are supported on pilotis, connected by bridges and accessed by a central stair and lifts. Each embassy is arranged on one floor in two parallel blocks connected by bridges, which allows the floors to have different sizes. Enclosures housing communal facilities are scattered beneath. Floating above is a sinuous concrete shell roof, which shields the building from the sun and monsoons. The disposition of elements defines and encloses a central courtyard, ventilated naturally by thermal stack effect and differential wind pressure, to provide a cool, comfortable space for public events and circulation, and to reduce the demands on the air conditioning system.

The buildings are orientated along an east–west axis to screen the main façades from a vertical midday sun. The two short façades, which enclose the courtyard, are designed so that the east elevation is open to the cool morning sun while the west elevation acts as a baffle to the intense midday and afternoon sun. The site and courtyard are informally landscaped with indigenous plants and trees.

The building services employ robust, easily maintained mechanical and electrical systems, which are integrated with passive solar control, solar collectors and bore hole water to provide a low energy building. The building and its services are designed to European standards and adapted to local conditions.

completion	November 2002
client	Foreign and Commonwealth Office, Estate Strategy Unit
area	6982 square metres/75,150 square feet
materials	Concrete shell roof, powder-coated aluminium louvres, bomb blast glazing
opposite	Aerial view from south, looking out to sea
top	East façade, main entrance and Visa Consular building
bottom	View looking northeast at east façade
photography	Peter Cook/View

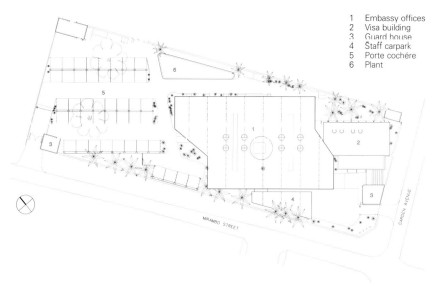

1 Embassy offices
2 Visa building
3 Guard house
4 Staff carpark
5 Porte cochére
6 Plant

opposite   Looking beyond pedestrian entrance at east
            elevation
top   East elevation onto the street
right   Site plan
photography Peter Cook/View

above	Internal view of circular rooflight and
	escape stair
opposite top	Section BB
opposite bottom	View across atrium looking east
opposite right	View towards east façade
photography	Peter Cook/View

Public

150 **Honan-Allston Branch of the Boston Public Library**
Machado and Silvetti Associates

164 **Reihoku Community Hall**
Hitoshi Abe, Yasuaki Onoda,
Atelier Hitoshi Abe

178 **The Richard B. Fisher Center for the Performing Arts at Bard College**
Gehry Partners LLP

154 **León Auditorium**
Mansilla + Tuñón Architects

166 **Rosenthal Center for Contemporary Art**
Zaha Hadid Architects

182 **Walt Disney Concert Hall**
Gehry Partners LLP

158 **Médiathèque**
Du Besset-Lyon architectes

170 **Stevie Eller Dance Theatre**
Gould Evans

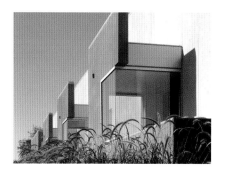

186 **Westchester-Loyola Village Branch Library**
Aleks Istanbullu Architects

162 **Niccolò Paganini Auditorium**
Renzo Piano Building Workshop

174 **STUK Arts Centre**
Neutelings Riedijk Architecten

188 **Williamsburg Community Center**
Pasanella + Klein Stolzman +
Berg Architects

Airport Cologne/Bonn
Germany
Murphy/Jahn, Inc.

Cologne Airport was built in the 1950s, and had become somewhat obsolete by the 1990s. In 1992, an international competition lead to Murphy/Jahn's commission for Terminal 2, a two-level roadway structure, Parkhaus (car parks) 2 and 3 and an underground train station.

Terminal 2 follows the leg of the splayed, layered 'U' configuration of the existing terminal. Its low profile extends the horizontality of the existing building. Whereas the existing building is of concrete and solid, the new building is constructed of prefabricated steel and glass components on an exposed concrete substructure, creating a light and transparent appearance.

The linear concourse is simple and easy to navigate. Routes to and from the Parkhaus 2, the elevated roadway or the train station and the planes also facilitate passenger movement.

The building consists of a structural module of 30 x 30 metre (98 x 98 foot) steel trees supporting a continuously folded roof plate with north-facing skylights. The roof consists of cells, placed onto the folded plate with simple bolted connections and waterproof joint seals. The cells are designed to fulfill various functions such as: light transmission, weather barrier, exterior heat absorption, interior heat absorption, acoustic dampening and absorption, and smoke ventilation.

The façade is a lightweight cable-supported steel and glass structure. The insulating glass panels are held by 'spiders' at their joints. Similar advanced lightweight and glass technologies are applied to the glass railings, elevators, fixed and moveable jet bridges, and glass floors and stairs.

The long sides of the parking structures are clad in stretched panels of stainless steel mesh. Based on lighting conditions their appearance varies from opaque to transparent, generating wonderful effects while passing through it, or driving by it. The large floor plates are punctuated by light courts to achieve natural ventilation and provide daylight.

completion	2001
area	69,000 square metres/742,700 square feet
structure	Exposed concrete
materials	Prefabricated steel systems, glass
awards	Deutscher Stahlbau Award 2002
opposite	Airside with jet bridges
top	30 m x 30 m structural tree
bottom	Ticketing hall with diagonal roof trusses
photography	HG Esch

above   Airside
bottom left Departures level
bottom right Hold area/boarding seating
opposite   Lower level arrivals
photography HG Esch

eBo Exhibition Pavilion
Bologna, Italy
MCA – Mario Cucinella Architects

This exhibition pavilion is located in the central piazza in Bologna and houses an exhibition of all the latest infrastructure projects being undertaken in the city. In order to contain the size of the building in such a sensitive historical context, it was decided to reuse an abandoned underground shopping area for the main exhibition of 800 square metres (8610 square feet) and to build two small glass pavilions at street level (100 square metres/1075 square feet each). The two pavilions are conceived as 'droplets' and sit raised slightly above the piazza level. They are clad with a double skin: the outer skin is curved clear glass and the inner skin is made up of transparent vertical Plexiglas tubes. During the day, when natural light shines on the tubes, the façade appears to vibrate. At night coloured lights inside the tubes transforms the droplets into two pulsating forms.

completion	2003
area	800 square metres/8610 square feet (main pavilion)
	200 square metres/2150 square feet (two smaller pavilions)
structure	Glass, Plexiglas
cost	EUR1.6 million
opposite left	View of eBo pavilions in Piazza Re Enzo
opposite right	View of curved glass external wall
opposite bottom	Night view of exterior
right	Detail of pavilion with ventilation ducts positioned on the floor between external curved glass wall and internal skin in Plexiglas tubing with rose LEDs positioned in each tube
bottom left	View of stairwell from pavilions, leading to underground exhibition space
bottom right	Entrance to pavilions with glass door and bamboo handle
photography	Jean De Calan

Federation Square
Melbourne, Victoria, Australia
Lab architecture studio in association with Bates Smart

Federation Square is the creation of a new urban order on a site that has never before existed. More than just a new set of buildings, Federation Square is now the centre of cultural activity for Melbourne. Fulfilling the long-held dream for a large, open public gathering space in Melbourne, Federation Square gives the citizens of Victoria an authentic civic destination. In the true spirit of federation, this design brings together distinct elements and activities that form a complex ensemble based upon the collective and the unique.

The project, 3.6 hectares (9 acres) in area and effectively the construction of an entire city block over railway tracks, consists of nine separate cultural and commercial buildings with a combined area of 45,000 square metres (484,400 square feet). These facilities include two new cultural institutions, Australian art galleries for the National Gallery of Victoria (NGVA) and the Australian Centre for the Moving Image (ACMI) grouped around two new civic spaces. One is a plaza capable of accommodating up to 35,000 people in an open-air amphitheatre, while the other is a unique glazed and covered atrium, whose southern end includes a glass-walled theatre. The overall facilities of the site also include the Melbourne headquarters of SBS, Australia's unique multi-cultural broadcaster, the Melbourne Visitors Information Centre, a function space, retail spaces, a car park and numerous restaurants and cafés.

Within an architecture of difference and coherence, the design has brought together these disparate institutions and allowed their true differences to be registered in the developed geometries, while also maintaining a visual and formal coherence across the site. Importantly, the design has also sought to produce a cultural and civic precinct based on permeability, allowing for the interaction of visitors, precinct workers and passersby.

opposite	Aerial view of Federation Square looking northeast
photography	courtesy Lab + Bates Smart
top	View across plaza. Buildings left to right: ACMI, atrium, Crossbar
photography	Peter Clarke
bottom	NGVA south façade
photography	Trevor Mein

completion   November 2002

client   State Government of Victoria and The City of Melbourne, delivered by the Office of Major Projects (1996–2000) and Federation Square Management (2000–present)

area   45,000 square metres/484,400 square feet

materials (exterior)   Façades: zinc (perforated and solid), Kimberly sandstone, translucent glass; structural deck: concrete slab; plaza: Kimberly sandstone; atrium: galvanised steel frame, glass panels

materials (interiors)   NGVA: pink and grey recycled ironbark flooring, precast polished concrete tiles, Kimberly sandstone pavers; ACMI: zinc and glass arcade, grey sandstone foyer flooring

cost $AUD475 million

top   Australian Centre for the Moving Image (ACMI), Flinders Street frontage

photography   Trevor Mein

above right   BMW Edge (south atrium) at night

photography   Peter Clarke

right   NGVA temporary exhibitions gallery

photography   Shannon Pawsey

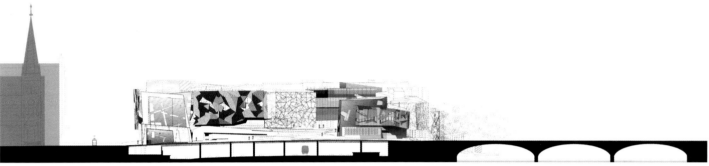

awards   International:
FX International Interior Design Awards
2003, London: Best museum/ gallery or
permanent exhibition category
Architecture + Cityscape Awards 2003,
Dubai: urban design category
Kenneth Brown Award 2003, Hawaii
(honourable mention)
National:
RAIA National Awards 2003: Walter Burley
Griffin Award for urban design
Interior Architecture Award
Dulux Colour Awards 2003: public spaces
and temporary structures award
Public Domain Awards 2003: sustainability
category
Sorel Awards 2001
Local:
RAIA Victorian Chapter Awards 2003:
Victorian Architecture Medal
The Melbourne Prize
Joseph Reed Award for urban design
Marion Mahony Award for interior
architecture
Award: Institutional New
Victorian Tourism Award 2003: general
tourism services

opposite   NGVA north intrafilament
photography   Shannon Pawsey
top left   View across plaza on new year's eve.
Buildings left to right: ACMI, atrium,
Crossbar.
photography   Peter Clarke
top right   BMW Edge interior (south atrium)
photography   Andrew Hobbs
above   West elevation
right   NGVA 20th Century art gallery
photography   Shannon Pawsey

First Nations Garden Pavilion, Montreal Botanical Garden
Montreal, Quebec, Canada
Saucier + Perrotte Architects

The First Nations Garden is a permanent commemoration of the great peace of Montreal of 1701. It is a crossroads of cultures, designed to help non-Native residents and visitors to discover the culture of the first inhabitants of North America. It also offers an opportunity for the First Nations to share their traditions, wisdom and knowledge.

Sheltering less than two per cent of the garden grounds, the pavilion is mostly outdoor space. Built along the garden's main pathway, the pavilion metaphorically raises the path to reveal the cultural memory of the place. The undulating roof recalls a wisp of smoke through the trees. Outdoor displays sheltered by the roof are framed by two indoor spaces at opposite ends of the pavilion – exhibition and orientation spaces at one end, public washrooms and a meeting space at the other. The pavilion also houses a boutique and offices.

The relationship between building and site, and the environmental sensitivity needed to maintain the spirit of the garden, was critical to the design of the pavilion. The new building acts as both a filter and a link between two key garden environments: a spruce and a maple forest. Wherever possible, the pavilion's exhibition program was moved outdoors. These exterior spaces orient the visitor and help to reduce the apparent size of the building by integrating the exhibition with the wider environment.

Vertical surfaces are minimised, limiting the visual impact of the building on the environment, and half of the built spaces are located underground to further reduce the influence of the new building on the existing setting. Materials have been selected for long life, chemical stability and suitability for re-use. Poured-in-place concrete, wood and weathering steel help to ground the pavilion in the landscape.

completion	2001
client	City of Montreal
area	418 square metres/4500 square feet (building); 19,970 square metres/215,000 square feet (garden)
structure	Cast-in-place concrete
cost	CAD$2.75 million (landscape, building, museology)
awards	OAQ Award of Excellence in Institutional Architecture 2003
	Governor General's Medal of Merit in Architecture 2002
	Canadian Architect Award of Excellence 2000
opposite	View from south
top	Outdoor exhibition space
bottom	Boutique's north elevation
photography	Marc Cramer

right   Outdoor exhibition space
bottom   Ground level plan and lower level plan
opposite left   Exterior showcases
opposite right   Service area
opposite bottom   Exterior showcases
photography   Marc Cramer

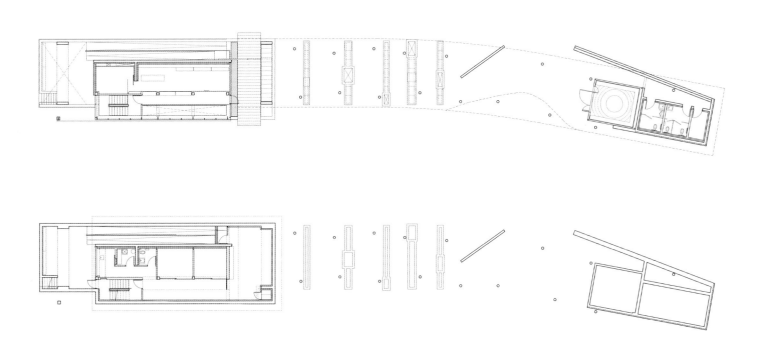

Honan-Allston Branch of the Boston Public Library

Allston, Massachusetts, USA

Machado and Silvetti Associates

The new Honan-Allston Branch of the Boston Public Library is one of 27 branches that provide an important outreach to Boston's neighbourhoods. Historically, this building type has been characterised by a casual, democratic expression, a latent tendency that was reinforced by the library's site along a heavily trafficked thoroughfare lined with wood residences, brick warehouses, and scattered commercial buildings. The client also placed specific demands on the building, among them requirements for a separate entry for community use and a one-storey configuration to maximise visual supervision on the inside. Responding to these various conditions, the 20,000-square-foot building's parti is divided into three parallel bands aligning with the main street – two 'solid' zones and one central void. The front zone contains all the active, information-gathering program components, including the stacks. The rear zone contains all the meeting spaces, which have after-hours community use. The middle zone is transparent, with alternating gardens and glass pavilion reading rooms. On the front of the library, the periodicals reading room is treated as a double-height additive piece that emphasises the institution's importance through its scale and rich palette, which includes slate panels, shingles, and rough sculpings. The library reaffirms a sense of urbanity by opening towards the street with a long horizontal band of windows. Passing through the front entrance, patrons arrive at a vantage-point where the organisation of the entire library unfolds before them, discovering the three inner gardens at the heart of the building.

completion	June 2001
client	Boston Public Library
	City of Boston, Public Facilities Department
area	1860 square metres/20,000 square feet
structure	Steel
materials	Norwegian slate panels, Vermont slate shingles and rough sculpings, jarrah cladding, wood windows, African mahogany casework, cork floors
cost	USD$6.5 million
opposite	View of reading room from North Harvard Street
top	Plan showing alternating gardens and reading rooms at centre
bottom	View of reading room and library entrance
photography	Michael Moran

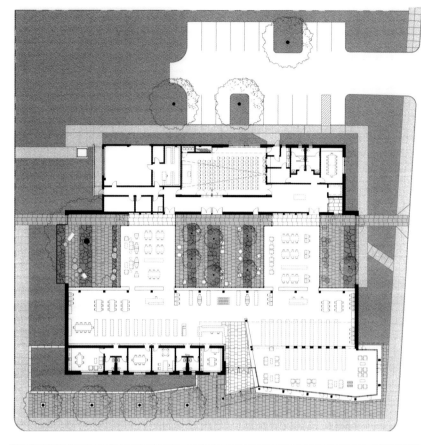

awards — National Honor Award, American Institute of Architects, 2003
Harleston Parker Medal 2003 (Boston Society of Architects + City of Boston)
Honor Award 2002, New England Chapter of the American Institute of Architects
Honor Award 2002, Boston Society of Architects
Honor Award 2002, Boston Society of Landscape Architects

right — Main reading room from front entrance

bottom — View from children's reading garden towards children's reading room and adult garden

opposite top — View of main reading room showing Norwegian slate panels

opposite middle — Section through the three gardens and two reading rooms

opposite bottom — View of the building's front from North Harvard Street

photography — Michael Moran

León Auditorium
León, Spain
Mansilla + Tuñón Architects

The Léon Auditorium pays homage to the
Ortega y Gasset-based 'see and be seen'
concept, and responds to the model
established by the splendid Manuel de Falla
auditorium in Granada. It is an exercise in
realism whose small size is not only a study
in usage and economics, but also reduces
its presence in the city. The concert hall
occupies the south side of a landscaped
plaza that also accommodates the 16th-
century San Marcos monastery, now a
luxury hotel.

The brilliant white façade is constructed as
a stack of windows with two distinct
appearances: the perimeter of the outer
apertures that refers to geometry, and the
inner aperture of each window, reflecting
the interior of the building. The five
horizontal bands that house the windows
increase in size as they rise towards the
top. Each window is a different size and
shape, but each is the result of carefully
calculated geometry. An eye-catching
display of large graphics runs along the
base of the façade.

In addition to the concert hall, the building
houses administrative offices, a triple-height
exhibition hall, foyer, public café, rehearsal
and dressing rooms, and technical and
service areas.

The concert hall is divided into two areas,
with seating for 734 patrons placed in front
of the stage, and a further 394 seats behind
it, allowing flexible configuration for large
symphony concerts and operas and smaller
chamber music events. The dark wenge
wood lining of the concert hall results in a
grand, but intimate, atmosphere.

completion	2002
client	Junta de Castilla y León, Ayuntamiento de León
area	9000 square metres/96,880 square feet
materials	White concrete, Roman travertine, aluminium roofing, wenge and oak wood
awards	Premio Aquitectura Española 2003
opposite	Exterior view
top	Exterior view
bottom	Night view
photography	Luis Asín

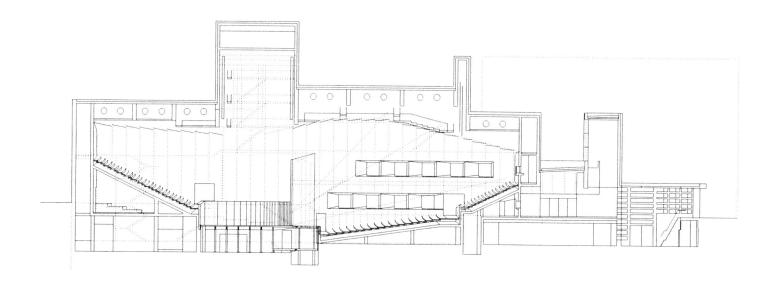

top   Section
bottom   Stage
opposite   Main lobby
photography   Luis Asín

Médiathèque
Troyes, France
Du Besset-Lyon architectes

The unflattering siting of the Troyes public library, to the rear of a Macdonald's restaurant, is in stark contrast to the importance of the collection of national treasures housed inside. The location led the architects to concentrate on the interior of the building, so as not to compete or even interact with the surrounding buildings. The geometry of the building is deliberately uncertain and elusive; the exterior makes no statement, and the distinctions between interior and exterior are deliberately blurred.

The library incorporates a main public area, information counter, children's library with story-telling space; book storage on three levels with fire-proof glass façade, a cafeteria, a glass-walled historical collection surrounded by ramps and a viewing platform, reading rooms and administrative offices.

The interior forms its own urban landscape with the incorporation of large-scale elements, and effectively negates any sense of the external environment. One of these dominant elements is a glittering, gold-coloured, undulating steel mesh suspended false ceiling, which covers the entire first floor. A pink staircase is immediately apparent once inside the plain façade. Yet another element is an artwork text by Lawrence Weiner that appears on the yellow glazing separating the children's reading zone from the ground floor corridor. The blue text is over 50 metres (165 feet) long and relates to the connection between writing and objects ('written in the heart of objects').

These oversize elements create a sense of openness. Far from overwhelming, they are transparent and colourful in nature and add to the overall impression of substance and depth; their size encourages visitors to explore and walk around them in order to appreciate them fully. The architects' desire is that this exploration and the acquired impressions will serve as a metaphor for reading.

completion	December 2002
client	Communauté d'Agglommération Troyenne
area	10,700 square metres/115,200 square feet
cost	EUR11,810,000
materials	Concrete structure, steel trusses, glass and aluminium façades, corrugated aluminium and polycarbonate sheet roofing; glass and aluminium partition walls and fire-proof walls; aluminium grid suspended ceilings on ground floor; curved suspended ceiling in aluminium profiles on first floor; floor coverings in carpeting, PVC, rubber and wood
opposite	Blue 'screen-façade' facing east
top	Entrance to médiathèque under canopy
middle	South and east façades
bottom	Main façade shows depth of building
photography	Philippe Ruault

awards	Groupe Moniteur Equerre d'argent, Best Building of the Year 2002
opposite top left and left	Corridor with pink stairway and artwork text on glass
opposite top right	Pink stairway
opposite bottom	Reading room on first floor under golden canopy
top	Old wooden reading room on first floor
photography	Philippe Ruault

Niccolò Paganini Auditorium

Parma, Italy
Renzo Piano Building Workshop

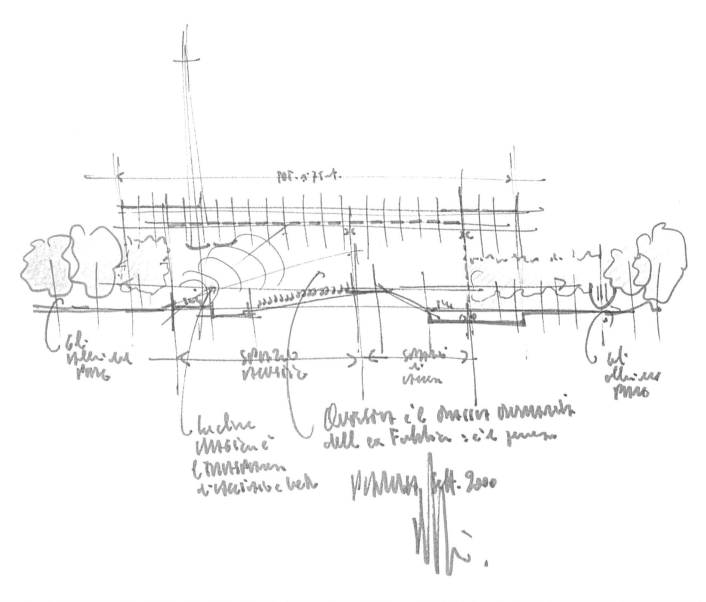

The Paganini Auditorium was built on the site of the disused Eridania sugar factory, a group of industrial buildings of vastly differing volumes and structures. Close to the historical centre of Parma, it is located in a now well-established park.

The size of the main building was an important factor in the conversion of the site to an auditorium. It was large enough to house a foyer, hall and stage, and also to meet basic acoustic requirements. Its location in the park simplified any required soundproofing needs, and the layout of the other factory buildings was suitable for other uses such as service and rehearsal spaces. The original brick exterior of the buildings was left largely untouched.

The project included removing the main building's transverse curtain walls, and replacing them with three large glass walls, to ensure transparency throughout the length of the 90-metre-long building. Even during concerts, the park can be seen from any point in the hall and foyer. A system of soundproof panels hung from the trusses over the stage completes the spatial organisation of the main body.

The public enters through the south end, and proceeds through the building's length. A roofed open-air space leads inside, passing through the first wide glass wall. From here one continues on to the two-level foyer. Located at the north end, near the glass end-wall, the 250-square-metre stage offers enough space for large musical ensembles that include a choir and orchestra. The gently sloping stalls cover an area of 590 square metres and seat 780 people, with good visibility from all rows.

completion	2001
client	City of Parma
cost	EUR14 million
opposite top	Architect's sketch
opposite left	Night view of auditorium
opposite right	Entrance to auditorium towards covered plaza and foyer
top	Two-level foyer houses reception, ticket office and cloakroom at lower level; upper level is reached by wide staircase or lift
bottom	Section
photography	Cano Enrico

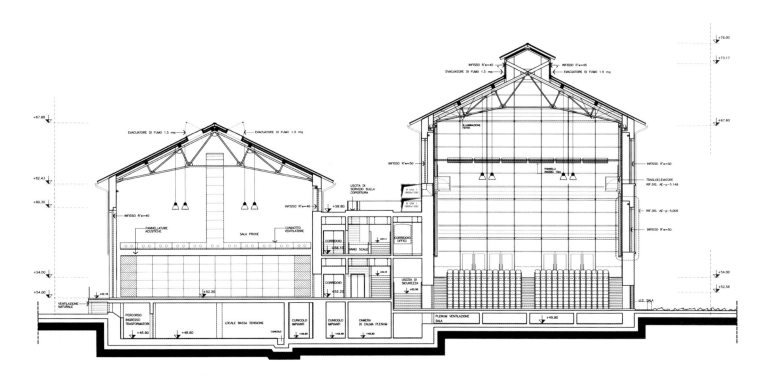

Reihoku Community Hall
Kumamoto, Japan
Hitoshi Abe, Yasuaki Onoda, Atelier Hitoshi Abe

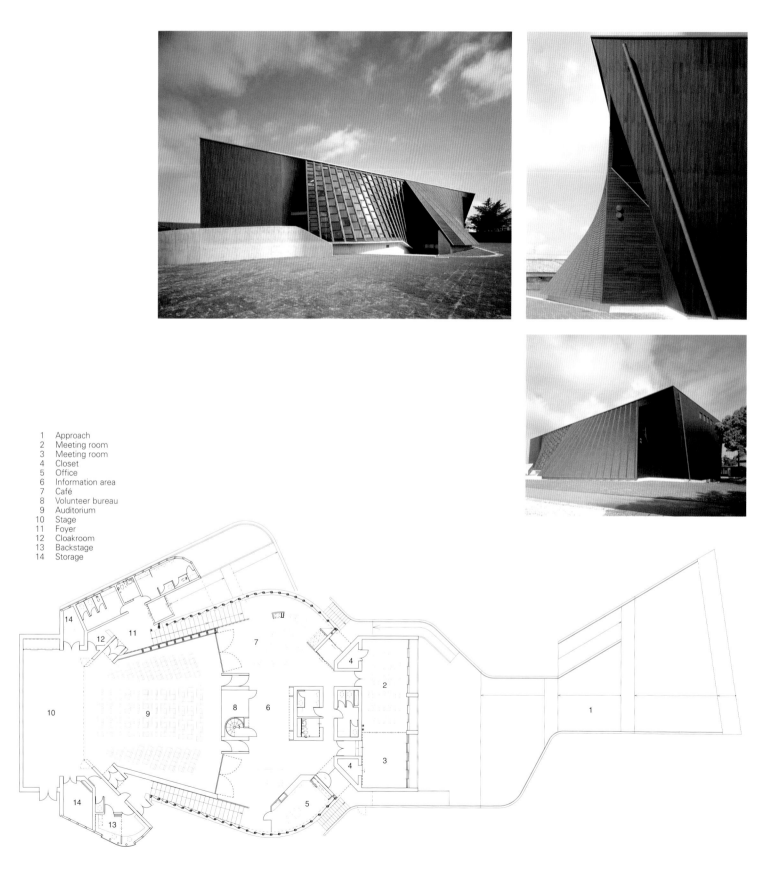

1 Approach
2 Meeting room
3 Meeting room
4 Closet
5 Office
6 Information area
7 Café
8 Volunteer bureau
9 Auditorium
10 Stage
11 Foyer
12 Cloakroom
13 Backstage
14 Storage

The 993-square-metre community centre is conceptually a simple box. What makes it unique are the two long, twisting, exterior walls, clad in dark cedar and glittering glass. The walls create an unexpected shape by unifying the diverse elements of the building, and help to relate an essentially geometric form to the surrounding natural topography. The unusual building has been embraced by the local community and has become a destination for architectural sightseers.

The non-load-bearing walls are comprised of 900 mm-wide (35-inch) glazed panels, bracketed by laminated timber verticals and horizontal cedar supports. The four entrances to the centre are hidden within the folds of the walls, which also have an acoustic function. The undulating folds and twists of the exterior walls are echoed by the winding internal staircase between the walls and the auditorium shell.

The centre contains a 207-seat auditorium at the northern end and two community meeting rooms at the southern end. A volunteer bureau, café, information area, offices, and kitchen facilities are included in the space between. Moveable partitions allow the theatre to be opened completely to the communal central spaces. A transitional indoor/outdoor space adjacent to the meeting rooms reinforces the interior/exterior nature of the building. Financial concerns dictated compact size of the building, and the choice of locally grown cedar as the principal material used in the structure.

completion	March 2002
client	Town of Reihoku, Kumamoto, Japan
area	993 square metres/10,700 square feet (floor area)
structure	Cedar (laminated timber), reinforced concrete base, glass
awards	Architectural Institute of Japan (AIJ) Award 2003
opposite top left	General view from east
opposite top right	View of north façade
opposite middle	General view
opposite bottom	First floor plan
top left	Stairway
top right	Opening door leads from theatre to café
middle	Café
bottom	Theatre and its extensive space
photography	Daici Ano

Rosenthal Center for Contemporary Art

Cincinnati, Ohio, USA
Zaha Hadid Architects

The Contemporary Arts Center was founded in Cincinnati in 1939 as one of the first institutions in the United States dedicated to the contemporary visual arts. The new CAC building provides spaces for temporary exhibitions, site-specific installations, and performances, but not for a permanent collection. Other program elements include an education facility, offices, art preparation areas, a museum store, a café and public areas.

The aim of the new building is to draw in pedestrians from the surrounding areas and create a sense of dynamic public space. The entrance and lobby lead in to the circulation system organised as an 'urban carpet'. Starting at the corner of Sixth and Walnut Street, the ground curves slowly upward as it enters the building, rising to become the back wall. As it rises and turns, this urban carpet leads visitors up a suspended mezzanine ramp through the full length of the lobby, which during the day functions as an open, day-lit landscape or an artificial park. The mezzanine ramp rises and penetrates the back wall.

On the other side it becomes a landing at the entrance to the galleries. In contrast to the urban carpet, which is a series of polished, undulating surfaces, the galleries are expressed as if they had been carved from a single block of concrete and were floating over the lobby space.

Views into the galleries from the circulation system are unpredictable, as the stair-ramp zigzags upward through a narrow slit at the back of the building. Together, these varying galleries interlock like a three-dimensional jigsaw puzzle, made up of solids and voids. The building's corner situation led to the development of two different, but complementary façades. The south façade forms an undulating, translucent skin, through which passersby see into the life of the Center. The east façade is expressed as a sculptural relief. It provides an imprint, the negative of the gallery interiors.

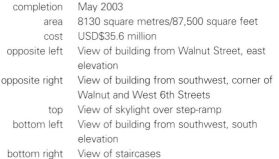

completion	May 2003
area	8130 square metres/87,500 square feet
cost	USD$35.6 million
opposite left	View of building from Walnut Street, east elevation
opposite right	View of building from southwest, corner of Walnut and West 6th Streets
top	View of skylight over step-ramp
bottom left	View of building from southwest, south elevation
bottom right	View of staircases
photography	Hélène Binet

opposite   View of exhibition space and step-ramp,
               fourth floor
top left   View of step-ramp, fourth floor
top right   Entrance hall, view of staircase with urban
               carpet
photography   Hélène Binet

Stevie Eller Dance Theatre

Tucson, Arizona, USA
Gould Evans

The spaces and forms for dance are about movement. The massing of the building is simple. The house and stage are black performance boxes. The dance studio is a glass box on the second floor that cracks away from the performance box. The dance studio is supported by columns that are neither straight nor of the same size nor located on a Cartesian grid. They are 'dancing columns' derived from *labanotation*, the graphically depicted movement score, of George Balanchine's *Serenade*, the first ballet for students at the newly founded American Ballet in New York City in 1934.

The crack between the dance studio and the performance boxes is a void, a space with a grated steel catwalk that is open to the lobby below. The box office is on wheels and transforms from box office to concession box to billboard. It moves from the inside lobby to the outside lobby.

The restrooms are white. Mirrors are imbedded in the ceramic tile and reflect the colours of clothing. Always moving, always changing.

An interior sound-reflective surface creates the volume of the house. It rolls and becomes an exterior surface that is a scrim; a *cyclorama* that can be transparent or opaque depending on the light. Just as the stage is a void upon which a performance is played, the black boxes of the house and stage create a similar void upon which the scrim pieces play.

completion	July 2003
client	University of Arizona
area	2660 square metres/28,600 square feet
structure	Stained CMU, steel, curtain wall
materials	Woven wire mesh fabric, knoll 'chroma' fabric on theatre seats, iron-infused interior paint for the house walls, exterior plaster, cast glass, sandblasted glass, aluminium floor grating, ground concrete floors, carpet
cost	USD$9 million
awards	AIA Arizona chapter Merit award 2003 Western Mountain Region AIA Honor award 2003 Best of 2003 – Best Public Building above $5 million, Southwest Contractor, 2003 2004 Merit Award in Architecture, US Institute for Theatre Technology
opposite	East elevation reveals woven wire fabric scrim surface
top	Detail scrim as wall and ceiling/dancing columns; mobile box office
bottom	Middle section
photography	Timothy Hursley

top   Inhabiting the space between scrim and black boxes, second means of egress from the dance studio

right   Dressing rooms open onto a wellness garden to become an indoor/outdoor somatics space

opposite top   Perspective render: exterior surface transforming to interior volume

opposite bottom   Interior house volume unfolds, opening proscenium to audience

photography   Timothy Hursley

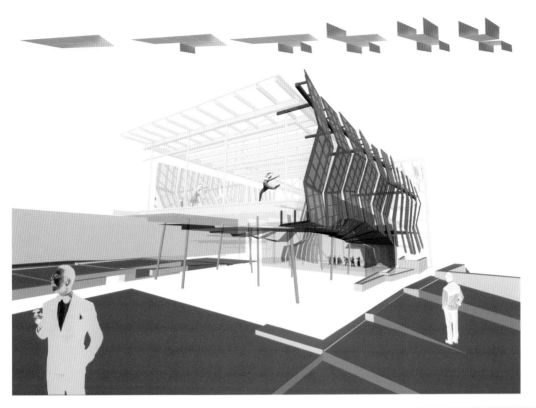

STUK Arts Centre
Leuven, Belgium
Neutelings Riedijk Architecten

For this project, the architects transformed the former Arenberg Institute at the University of Leuven into new accommodation for the STUK Arts Centre. The original Institute comprised a series of buildings around an inner court, most of which dated from the beginning of last century. The transformation involved demolition of two wings, radical makeover of two wings, and a slight face-lift of two wings. In addition, the exterior space has been completely revamped. The result is a complex that allows multiple use by all forms of performing arts, music and the visual arts.

The complex has ten large public theatres in addition to a number of large public reception areas, such as the café-restaurant and the foyer, and numerous 'behind the scenes' spaces. The patio, an intimate inner court, forms the complex's heart and point of orientation.

Each space within the STUK has a character all of its own in relation to ambience, finish, dimensions, light, view, and spatiality. As a result, a neutral, multifunctional complex has been avoided, and a kaleidoscopic labyrinth of distinctive locations has been created. A wide range of materials and finishes has been used, such as oiled concrete with a zigzag pattern in bas-relief, capped with brass rosettes; padded black leather walls fastened with shiny button-headed nuts; translucent slatted walls of rusty iron; masonry gold bars; black perforated shutters with red velvet filling; and crates of rough wood, all adding to the appealingly whimsical nature of the project.

The contrast between old and new is accentuated by the idiosyncratic sculptural volume structure of the new sections of the complex. The choice of red brick for the exterior of the new buildings unites the old and new sections.

completion	2002
client	STUK Arts Centre
area	10,000 square metres/107,600 square feet
cost	EUR6 million
opposite	Entrance patio is bordered by an enormous frame supported by the four STUK letters
top	View from internal patio
bottom	Theatre
photography	Sarah Blee Architectural Photography

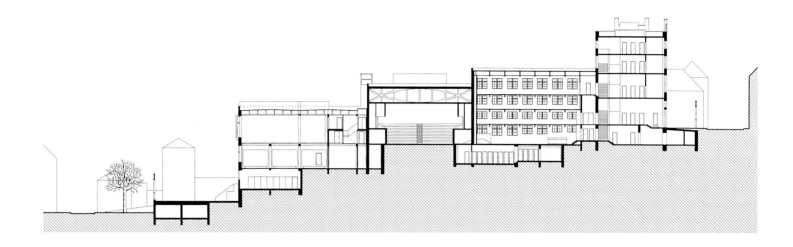

top   Section
above left   Music studio
above right Dance studio
opposite top View from rooftop
opposite bottom Foyer
photography Sarah Blee Architectural Photography

The Richard B. Fisher Center for the Performing Arts at Bard College
Annandale-on-Hudson, New York, USA
Gehry Partners LLP

The building, containing two multipurpose performance theatres, is located on the Bard College campus in a beautiful area of tall trees and open lawns.

The Sosnoff Theater is the primary performance space within the building. A concert shell and fore-stage lift allow conversion for symphonic music performance. It has 850 seats in an orchestra section and two balcony sections. By seating the audience only in the orchestra section, a feeling of intimacy is provided for smaller student productions intended for audiences of 400–500 people. By placing additional seating on the stage, the capacity can be increased to 920. The theatre features a wood ceiling and concert shell. The house walls are concrete, providing the mass necessary for excellent acoustical reflections. The highly sculptural exterior responds to the theatre's internal organisation. The stainless steel panels loosely wrap around the sides of the theatre toward the proscenium, creating two tall, skylit gathering areas on either side of the main lobby. The panels then flare out at the proscenium, creating a sculptural collar-like shape that rests on the simple concrete and plaster form of the stage house.

Theater 2 is a black-box theatre dedicated to student dance and drama productions, and can accommodate up to 300 seats. The seats are retractable, allowing reconfiguration into a large, open performance space. The interior is clad in solid and perforated painted plywood panels. The exterior features concrete and plaster walls and an undulating roof clad in stainless steel panels. Glazed skylights integrated into the roof and operable windows allow natural light and ventilation into the two dance and two drama rehearsal rooms. Administrative offices, conference rooms, and a secondary lobby and gathering area are also located adjacent to Theater 2.

A number of different exterior materials and finishes were considered for the building. After a lengthy on-site review process, a soft, brushed stainless steel was selected for the exterior cladding because of the material's ability to reflect the light and colours of the sky and the surrounding landscape.

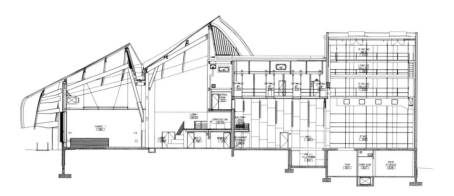

completion	2003
client	Bard College
area	9940 square metres/107,000 square feet
structure	Stainless steel panels, concrete, glass
opposite	Main entrance
top	Section of Theater Two, related support spaces, rehearsal room, and lobby
bottom	Exposed steel structure of the entry canopy continues into lobby of Sosnoff Theater
photography	Peter Aaron/Esto

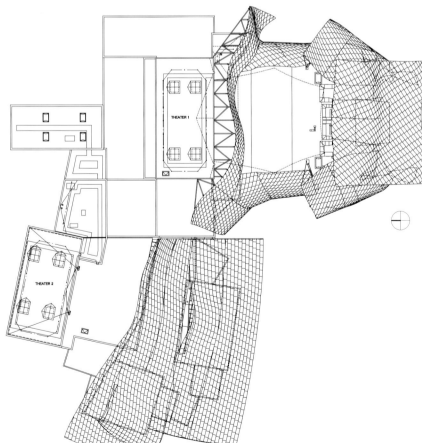

top   Gehry design sketch of Sosnoff Theater,
                view from audience seating towards stage
right   Roof plan of Sosnoff Theater, Theater Two
                and rehearsal rooms
opposite top   Sosnoff Theater, view from stage to
                audience seating
photography   Peter Aaron/Esto
opposite bottom Final design model of Theater Two, view
                from stage to audience seating
sketch and model Courtesy Gehry Partners LLP

Walt Disney Concert Hall
Los Angeles, California, USA
Gehry Partners LLP

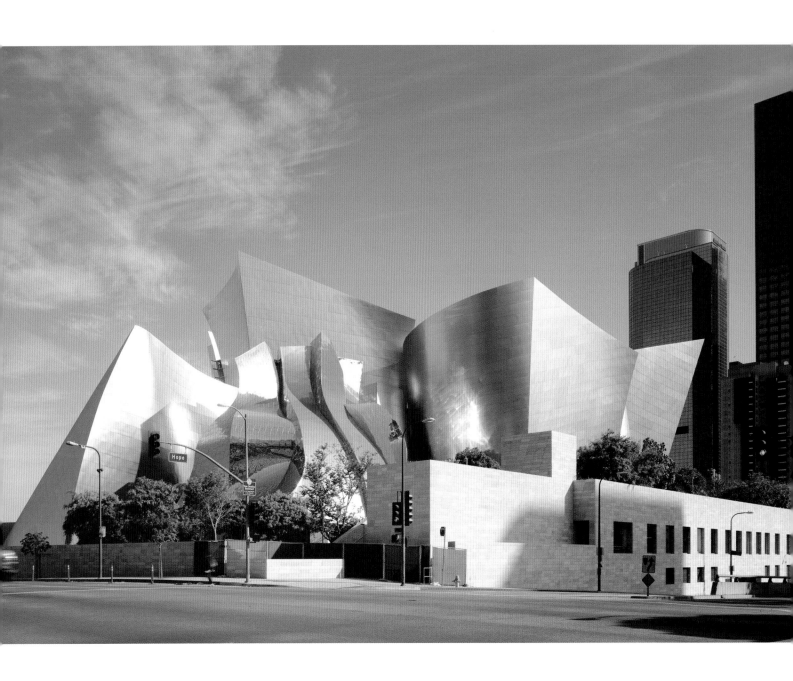

Located on a prominent site in downtown Los Angeles, the Walt Disney Concert Hall serves as the permanent home of the Los Angeles Philharmonic. The majority of the site is devoted to gardens, accessible from the concert hall and from adjacent streets. The concert hall lobby is accessible from the street; large operable glass panels provide maximum accessibility to various amenities including a gift shop, restaurant and café, an underground parking garage, and a pre-concert performance space, which will be used for performance-related lectures, educational programs, and other scheduled and impromptu performances. The focus of the design is the 2265-seat main concert hall, whose interior and form are a direct expression of acoustical parameters. Seating surrounds the orchestra platform. The wood walls and the sail-like wooden ceiling forms give one the impression of being within a great ship inside the walls of the hall. A pipe organ designed in conjunction with the interiors occupies a central position between the seating blocks at stage rear. Skylights and a large window at the rear of the hall allow natural light to enhance daytime concerts. The exterior of the concert hall is clad in stainless steel panels. The building's orientation, combined with the curving and folding exterior walls, presents highly sculptural compositions as viewers move along adjacent streets and through the surrounding gardens and plazas. An extensive backstage technical area surrounds the concert hall and opens onto a private garden for musicians. The Roy and Edna Disney 250-seat multi-use theatre for California Institute of the Arts (CalArts) programs is included in the base of the building. This facility, together with its separate lobby, art gallery and café, will be a major venue for CalArts in the city of Los Angeles. A six-level, 2500-car garage is located below grade with access from three surrounding streets.

completion	2003
client	Los Angeles Philharmonic
area	18,580 square metres/200,000 square feet
opposite	Highly sculptural forms in mirror-finish stainless steel
top	Exterior walkway detail
bottom	Final design model, view along Grand Avenue façade
photography	Grant Mudford
model	Courtesy Gehry Partners LLP

below left   Gehry design sketch depicting main entrance at Grand Avenue and First Street, as well as the Grand Avenue façade

below right   Main entrance at Grand Avenue and First Street, and Grand Avenue façade

bottom   Presentation axonometric depicting main entrance at Grand Avenue and First Street, and Grand Avenue façade

opposite top   Lobby; column clad in Douglas fir to right is both structural and conceals HVAC and lighting

opposite bottom   Main hall, from audience seating to stage. Of note is the fully functional organ, with over 6000 pipes, designed by Frank Gehry and organ designer Manuel Rosales.

photography   Grant Mudford

sketch and model   Courtesy Gehry Partners LLP

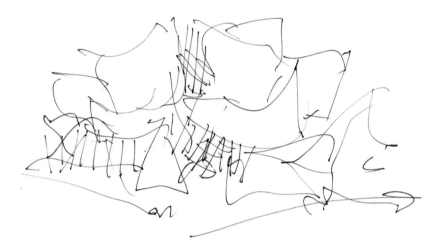

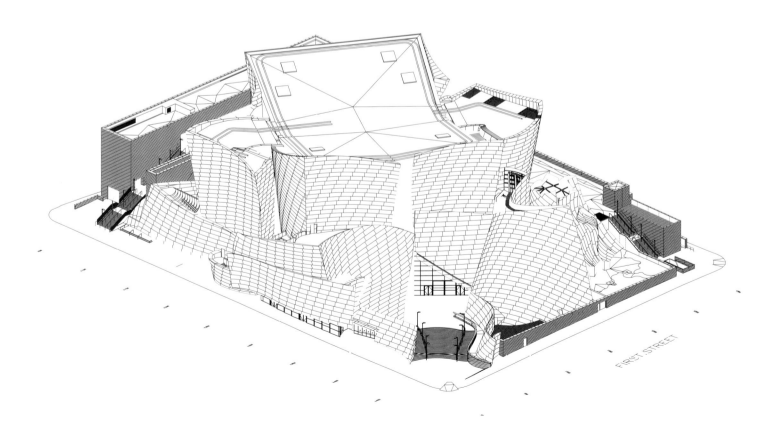

Westchester-Loyola Village Branch Library
Westchester, California, USA
Aleks Istanbullu Architects

The new building combines two branch libraries and serves 12 elementary schools, four junior high and high schools, and the large local population. Featuring open stacks, reading nooks, computer terminals, children's area, information desk, circulation desk, staff offices, and a meeting room, the new library is a civic building that meets diverse needs while providing a sense of intimacy for its users.

The site strategy was to create a large urban park to link the new community library with the existing Municipal Hall. The design incorporates state-of-the-art sustainable technologies such as solar collectors and storm-water retainage systems.

The building is an interplay of forms, both solid and transparent. Massive walls are punched with windows and insets. On the east side, four interior reading bays alternate with exterior planes holding small lava rocks.

From the park on the west side, a cantilevered aluminium-clad canopy leads to an intimately scaled foyer and the grand main hall. The double-height space runs laterally across the entire building. Large windows on either end afford clear views through the building from outside, reinforcing the play of interior and exterior. Visitors filter through increasingly dense and private reading areas to the stacks beyond. Bay windows behind the stacks connect private reading nooks to a serene view of a eucalyptus grove. The massing of the building and subtle variations in colour, texture, and reflectivity are designed to highlight and modulate the experience of the sequence of interior spaces.

Maple wood is the predominant material used to create a warm and receptive inner sanctum. The maple walls, ceilings, stacks, furniture, and circulation and information desks are a serene counterpoint to the dense orange accents and green carpeting. Aluminium is brought back inside on the tops of the desks and in the form of a great awning over the circulation desk.

Working in collaboration with the architect, artist Jill d'Angelica created a sequence of silk-screened portraits for the wood paneling based on interviews with neighbourhood people about their favourite books.

completion	2003
client	City of Los Angeles
area	1160 square metres/12,500 square feet
opposite	Bay windows with reading nooks
top	Double-height main hall
bottom	Lantern-like street presence
photography	Tom Bonner

Williamsburg Community Center

Brooklyn, New York, USA

Pasanella + Klein Stolzman + Berg Architects

The Community Center was built by the New York City Housing Authority as part of its program to renovate 24 residential buildings near the site.

Designed to serve neighbourhood children, youth, and adults for everyday use and special events, the Williamsburg Community Center has a varied program. It houses a gymnasium, dance studio, classrooms, art studios and darkroom, a computer room, a movie projection screen, stage, recording studio and other multipurpose spaces for neighbourhood use. In addition to the recreational areas, the Center also houses a commercial kitchen offering lunches to seniors year round and school children during summer months and enabling the Center to be rented out for weddings or other catered events.

The Community Center is composed of a series of pavilions that extend out from the large, central multipurpose space to engage the park site. These pavilions give the building an intimate, approachable scale and integrate the building with the life of the park and the neighbourhood. As a security precaution, the building's siting and configuration allow it to be partially or completely closed at any time, while transparent and semitransparent walls allow a visual connection between inside and out, giving a sense of control to the inhabitants. Its dematerialisation softens the boundary between the building's interior and exterior, making it lively and inviting, and providing a real connection to the neighbourhood. Inside the building, large, operable garage-like doors and moveable partitions create flexible program spaces.

completion	September 2003
client	New York City Housing Authority
area	1905 square metres/20,500 square feet
structure	Steel frame and panel infill system with reinforced glass, perforated aluminium screen, metal fencing
materials	Glass block, metal siding, Kalwall, heavy gauge wire mesh, concrete, ceramic mosaic tile
cost	USD$5.5 million
awards	International Interior Design Association, Best in Competition Award 2003 New York State Chapter of the American Institute of Architects, Award for Design Excellence, 1999
opposite	View of entrance from the intersection of Graham Avenue and Scholes Street
top	View of exterior façade along Graham Avenue
bottom	View through building to gymnasium and outdoor basketball court
photography	Paul Warchol

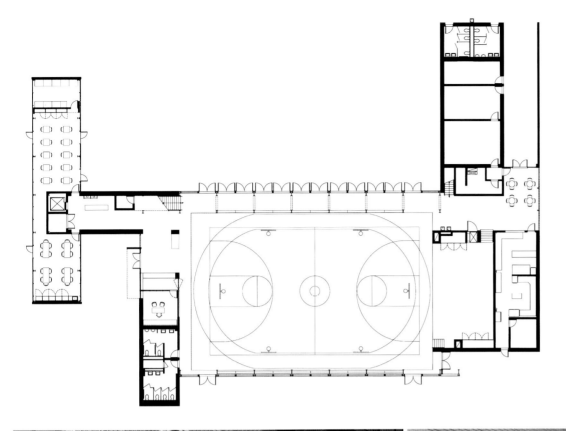

opposite   View from mezzanine lounge towards main
             stairwell and gymnasium
top   First floor plan
above left   View of gymnasium from entrance
above right View from gymnasium to entrance,
             mezzanine offices, and conference room
photography Paul Warchol

Residential

2.N.D. House

Cape Schanck, Victoria, Australia
Stephen Jolson

The 2.N.D House is a 372-square-metre, 4-bedroom residence located on the National Golf Course in Cape Schanck, Victoria, Australia. Contemporary factory-finished materials, including raw precast concrete, anodised aluminium, galvanised steel and glass form the external envelope.

The interior of the house has been designed with careful attention to detail. Plasterboard panels float in front of the precast concrete walls, and the solid bamboo flooring and joinery panels result in a continuous play of light and shadow. The colour palette of materials is derived from the local landscape.

From its inception, the house was designed with careful consideration of the surrounding rugged environment. The front and rear elevations address the point of arrival by car and the experience of golfers as they meander around the golf course. Upon arrival by car, the house is perceived as a series of monolithic concrete panels rising from the sandy slope. The entry chamber and concrete catwalk that signify the entrance are designed to slice the elements of the surrounding environment, framing a portion of the second hole tee-off, the native tea-trees, the ocean and the sky, presenting a 'frozen moment'.

From the golf course, the house is perceived as a series of horizontal planes floating amongst the tea-trees, expressing the lineal direction of the golf course 'drive'. Capped by galvanised steel channels, the strong horizontal roof and floor plates are intersected by the vertical slice of the concrete entry chamber. The views from the balcony are compressed by the cantilevered roof plates, through the glass balustrades of the balconies, which are designed as 'transparent barriers'. There are 18 'water exhaust outlets' in lieu of downpipes, which allow rainwater to cascade from the roof plates onto rock-covered erosion control pits below.

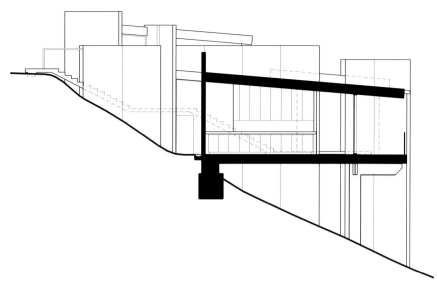

completion	March 2002
area	372 square metres/4000 square feet
structure	Precast concrete panels, galvanised steel, glass and anodised aluminium
materials	Plasterboard, 2-Pak paint, solid bamboo flooring and joinery panels
cost	AUD$1.5 million
awards	The Kevin Cavanagh Medal for Excellence in Concrete 2003 Awards
opposite	Catwalk entry at night
top	Section
bottom	Golfers' view of the house amongst the rugged landscape
photography	Scott Newett

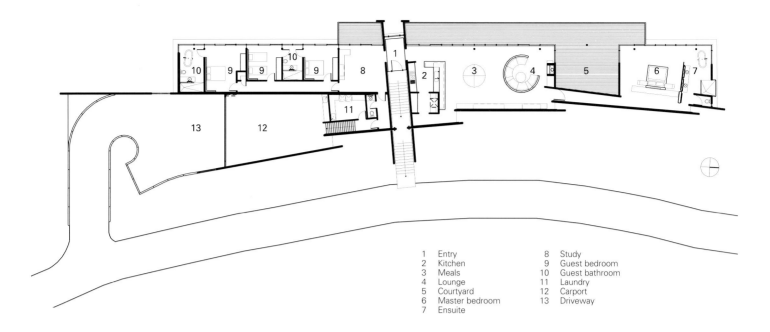

1	Entry	8	Study
2	Kitchen	9	Guest bedroom
3	Meals	10	Guest bathroom
4	Lounge	11	Laundry
5	Courtyard	12	Carport
6	Master bedroom	13	Driveway
7	Ensuite		

above	Floor plan
below	View along balcony
opposite left	Master ensuite shower with view into rugged landscape
opposite right	Catwalk entry into house
opposite bottom	Master bedroom joinery and bed
photography	Scott Newett

Colorado Court
Santa Monica, California, USA
Pugh Scarpa Kodama

Colorado Court is one of the first buildings of its type in the US that is 100 per cent energy neutral to the electrical grid. It incorporates energy efficient measures that exceed standard practice, optimise building performance, and ensure reduced energy use.

Planning and design emerged from close consideration and employment of passive solar design strategies that include: locating and orienting the building to control solar cooling loads, for exposure to prevailing winds, and to induce buoyancy for natural ventilation; designing windows to maximise daylighting and natural ventilation; shading south-facing windows and minimising west-facing glazing; shaping and planning the interior to enhance daylight and natural air flow distribution.

State-of-the-art technologies include a natural gas-powered turbine/heat recovery system that generates the base electrical load and hot water demands for the building and a solar electric panel system integrated into the façade and roof of the building that supplies most of the peak-load electricity demand. The co-generation system converts utility natural gas to electricity to meet the base load power needs of the building and captures waste heat to produce hot water for the building throughout the year as well as space heating needs in the winter. The solar photovoltaic panels are integral to the building envelope and unused solar electricity is delivered to the grid during the daytime and retrieved from the grid at night as needed. These systems will pay for themselves in less than ten years and annual savings in electricity and natural gas bills are estimated to be in excess of $6000.

completion	2002
client	Community Corporation of Santa Monica
area	2800 square metres/30,150 square feet
cost	USD$4.2 million
materials	Concrete masonry unit (CMU) face block, low-e dual glazing, bitumen membrane roofing, solar photovoltaic integrated wall panel system, recycled light gauge steel, galvanised sheet metal
opposite top	Overall view of the building from corner of 5th Street and Colorado Avenue
opposite left	Detail at the second floor bridge over main entry on 5th Street
opposite right	Detail of solar façade at the second floor courtyard
top	Overall view of building main entry on 5th Street
bottom	Early sketch showing overall building configuration
photography	Marvin Rand

awards	National AIA Design Award 2003
	AIACC Award 2003
	AIA/LA Award 2003
	Rudy Bruner Prize 2003
	World Habitat Award Finalist 2003
	AIA COTE 'Top Ten Green Building' Award 2003
	SCANPH 'Project of the Year'
	Westside Urban Prize 2002
	AIA PIA National Housing Award 2003
top	Detail at the second floor bridge over main entry on 5th Street
right	Stair detail showing translucent solar panels
opposite top	South-facing façade of upper court showing the building shade screen
opposite bottom	Ground floor plan
photography	Marvin Rand

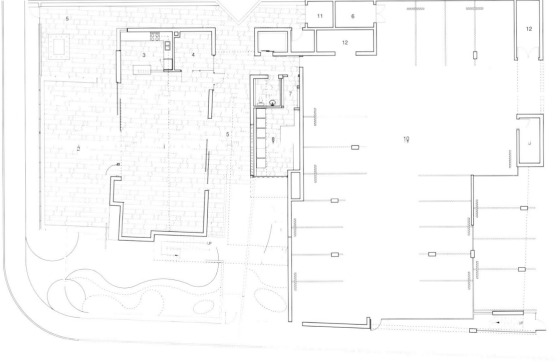

1   Lobby/Lounge
2   Common courtyard
3   Kitchen
4   Office
5   Entry
6   Storage room
7   Mail room
8   Laundry
9   Mechanical
10 Parking
11 Electrical room
12 Trash/recycling collection

Harmony Garden (JinLin-Yihe Residential Development)
Shanghai, PRC
Joseph Wong Design Associates (JWDA)

This charming housing community is the third phase of an expansive housing project located 20 minutes outside the city centre in Shanghai, China. It offers a variety of housing options to an increasingly wealthy and sophisticated population.

The gated community comprises four multi-storey, multi-family buildings offering 70 units and 125 attached and detached single family homes along the Heng Jin River. The name of the development, Yihe or Harmony Gardens, reflects the owner's desire to create a community that harmonises with nature, bringing the beauty of the natural world into the domestic domain.

The first site improvements were along the river bank, with the instalment of lush landscaping, a commodious walkway along the river, and the improvement of existing pedestrian bridges across the river. The old bridges were a motley assembly of poured concrete and simple construction. The new bridges evoke the rich cultural heritage of China and offer a pleasing vista to the detached single-family homes along the river.

The next step included the creation of an artificial river to flow through the development, giving some homes a palatial feel as one crosses the river to gain entrance and others a place for quiet reflection. The result is a space that is organic and evokes a slower and quieter pace of life like the Shanghai of yore. Other elements include clever T-shaped driveways for the attached single-family homes, eliminating the need for an extra right of way that would have robbed the site of some of the vital open space. The single family homes range from 340 to 698 square metres (3660 to 7510 square feet) and offer a variety of pleasing floor plans.

completion	January 2003
client	Yuan Sen Development Company, Shanghai
area	17,620 square metres/612,600 square foot
structure	Concrete, tile roof, stone veneer, wood-frame windows
materials	Plaster walls, wood doors, carpeted and wood floors
cost	USD$25 million
awards	National Housing Administration, China – Best Planning Award
opposite	View of development; detached single family homes with the Heng Jin River on right
top	Pedestrian walkway between attached single family homes with view of multi-storey, multi-family buildings to rear
bottom	Detached single family homes to left of road, artificial river, bridge in foreground; attached single family homes to right
photography	Kerun Ip

opposite   Large detached single family homes along Heng Jin River, river-side site improvements in foreground

top   Side-street access for attached single family homes

above   Artificial river; large detached single family homes to left and smaller attached single family homes to right

photography   Kerun Ip

Harvard University One Western Avenue
Allston, Massachusetts, USA
Machado and Silvetti Associates

One Western Avenue occupies a prominent site at the southeast corner of the Harvard Business School campus. Designed to house more than 350 occupants in 235 apartments, it will help relieve pressure on the area's private housing market. The project is part of the University's commitment to house more of its population and to contribute to the stability of the private housing market in Cambridge and Boston.

One Western Avenue combines two emblematic types of courtyard and mid-rise buildings, while adding a three-storey, bridge-like building raised four levels above the ground and spanning 180 feet. This bridge is very important and performs several tasks: first, it clearly divides the building's main open area into a courtyard and a front lawn; second, it creates a covered terrace between courtyard and front lawn; third, it allows a courtyard open to the river, and on the top of its edge, three stories of apartments occupying the same 'front-row' situation. Finally, from a formal architectural point of view, the newness of the bridge places the building squarely in the domain of the 21st century. Consistent with the choice of building types is the selection of skin materials: brick for the courtyard and cast stone for the mid-rise and the bridge. The courtyard building is wrapped in two brick patterns, one for the exterior walls and the other for the interior walls. These overlap in the entry passageway, thus producing a third pattern. The mid-rise and the bridge are clad in the same material, but used differently from one another, as are the types of windows they display.

completion	September 2003
client	Harvard Real Estate Services
area	21,660 square metres/200,000 square feet (housing)
	24,810 square metres/267,000 square feet (parking below grade)
structure	Steel
materials	Velour-textured brick with medium ironspot; cast stone in Tudor, split-face, and cloth finishes; aluminium windows and louvres; metal canopies; gypsum fibre-reinforced concrete panels (under bridge); Jarrah decking and benches
cost	USD$57 million (housing)
	USD$36 million (parking below grade)
opposite	View of building from the Charles River
top	View of intersection between mid-rise and low-rise buildings
bottom	View of bridge where it intersects low-rise building
photography	Michael Moran

top   View of portal on Western Avenue
right   View of wooden benches beneath bridge
opposite View of bridge and tower towards Charles
         River
photography Michael Moran

Natural Ellipse House
Tokyo, Japan
EDH+MIAS; Masaki Endoh + Masahiro Ikeda

The site for this unique house is on the edge of Shibuya, amongst the glaring, multicoloured neon lights of Tokyo's shopping and entertainment district. The geometry adopted for the building was that of the ellipse, a shape that can be modified by varying the ratio between its major and minor axes, in order to adjust its form to fit within external restrictions. The overall shape comprises 24 units of elliptical rings placed along a horizontal elliptical orbit. The steel frame was laser-cut in a factory that produces silos.

The cage-like steel frame is covered by a flexible skin of fibre-reinforced polymer (FRP), a waterproof material that can be easily moulded to create a seamless exterior and which also has special fire-resistant qualities. A roof-top glazed terrace, partially hidden by the indentation at the top of the structure, allows daylight into all levels of the house, via the spiral staircase. Some smaller openings appear at irregular intervals around the perimeter of the house, and allow views of neighbouring buildings. Inside, the staircase connects the four storeys and basement levels. All floors are painted concrete slabs, ceilings are painted steel plate and walls are painted mineral board.

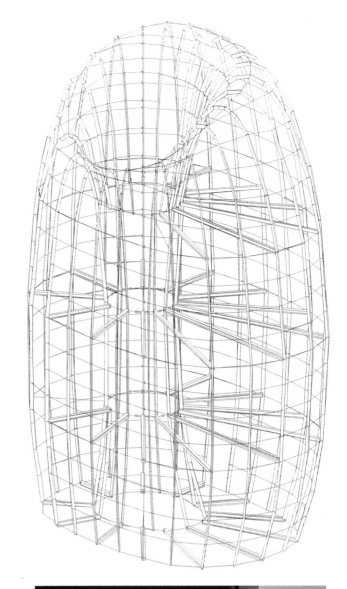

completion	June, 2002
area	132 square metres/1421 square feet
structure	Steel
materials	Non-flammable FRP waterproofing, oil paint finish, steel sash windows, steel plate ceilings, mineral board walls, concrete slab floors
awards	Japan Institute of Architects Rookie of the Year 2003
opposite	Evening view
top	Axonometric
right	Looking down staircase from terrace
bottom	Second floor
photography	Hiro Sakaguchi

Paranal Astronomers' Residence

Paranal, Atacama Desert, Chile

Paula Gutierrez Erlandsen – Arquitectura y Decoración

Paranal, in Chile's Atacama Desert is the site of the European Southern Observatory's Very Large Telescope (VLT) array, the world's largest and most advanced optical telescope. With its unprecedented optical resolution and unsurpassed surface area, the VLT produces extremely sharp images and can record light from the faintest and most remote objects in the Universe. Situated 2800 metres above sea level, and 1200 kilometres from Santiago, Paranal's unique climatic conditions of 350 days per year of clear day and night skies are ideal conditions for an astronomical observatory. It is also believed to be the driest area on Earth.

An architectural competition was held to design a residence for the scientists located at this remote site. The German firm Auer + Weber designed the building and the interiors were designed by Chilean architect Paula Gutierrez Erlandsen.

The main goal was to build a residence that blended with the desert surroundings. Because of the strict requirements in relation to light pollution, the residence is blacked out at 7pm each night, with extreme precautions taken not to allow any artificial light to escape and pollute the pristine observatory conditions. In this atmosphere of isolation and seclusion, the architects' goal was to make the residence as warm and welcoming as possible.

The residence comprises four floors, 110 individual apartments and common areas including reception, a 24-hour cafeteria, terraces, and two libraries. Several small interior gardens were designed to give the idea of open spaces, and the most impressive garden is a real oasis with palm trees and a tranquil central swimming pool. In contrast to the harsh terrain of the desert outside, the residence is comfortable, colourful, contemporary and functional.

completion	2002
client	European Southern Observatory (ESO)
area	10,000 square metres/107,600 square feet
materials	Concrete, crystal and opaque steel
opposite left	General view of reception area; artworks of Roberto Matta in background
opposite right	View of central space with tropical garden and electrically operated roof
opposite bottom	Contextual view of residence, telescopes and surrounding Atacama desert
top	Entrance view: the building blends seamlessly with the desert
bottom	Reading area
photography	Igor Almonacid

Silodam
Amsterdam, The Netherlands
MVRDV

A mixed program of 157 residences, offices, work spaces, commercial spaces and public spaces are arranged in a 20-metre-deep (60-foot), 10-storey-high building located on the IJ canal in Amsterdam. The building makes reference to the adjacent historical grain silos at the Silodam, and to the shipping containers stacked nearby, and in fact resembles a container ship with its colourful, stacked façade.

The building, erected on concrete pillars, includes a variety of different apartments, including patio apartments, studios, studio apartments, maisonettes and penthouses. Groups of 4–8 dwellings with identical layouts form 'little neighbourhoods' and are identified by the different uses of materials in their façades and also by the colours of their hallways and galleries.

The residences not only differ in size and position within the building, but also in interior layout, width, depth, construction, exterior spaces such as balconies and patios, floor heights, accessibility (by corridor, gallery, bridge or stairs), number of rooms, floor voids, and types of windows. Adding to the metropolitan character of the complex is a large, shared balcony for the residents.

The terrace is the end point of a public promenade with magnificent views along the IJ. Residents can walk through the building, passing different façades and roof tops, go through the heart of the building, or walk along the marina and the hall. The marina for residents is located beneath the building, between the supporting concrete columns.

completion	2002
client	Rabo Vastgoed, Utrecht, De Principaal bv, Amsterdam; Bouwcombinatie Graansilo's vof, Amsterdam
area	19,500 square metres/210,000 square feet
materials	Concrete, western red cedar, aluminium, glass, brick, steel, synthetic corrugated sheeting, Prodema
opposite	General view, with historic grain silo to right
top	Side view
bottom	Façade detail shows use of different materials to identify different internal uses
photography	Rob 't Hart Fotografie

right Corridor views
middle Architect's sketch
bottom View from IJ River
opposite Support structure in marina
photography Rob 't Hart Fotografie

Other

Apple Store

SoHo, New York, USA
Bohlin Cywinski Jackson

Apple Computer's new retail store in the heart of the SoHo shopping district occupies a 1920's former U.S. Post Office. The previously restored landmark exterior contrasts sharply with an ethereal interior, emphasising the refined design and elegant technology of Apple's products. The prototype Apple stores with maple floors, white fixtures, and integrated ceiling system, provide an opportunity for consumers to shop in an environment that supports a corporate identity associated with simplicity and good design.

The SoHo store expands on the prototype concept by incorporating two floors of retail space. The simple palette of the prototype was augmented by the addition of stone flooring, bead-blasted stainless steel panels, custom wood fixtures and laminated glass elements.

The vista of the double-storey interior space from the street offers a compelling invitation. The eye is drawn to the levitating glass staircase, bridge and skylight system. Cantilevered glass guardrails allow clear views of second floor spaces. The skylight, threaded by delicate stainless steel frames, admits natural light and glimpses of the surrounding roofs and cityscape.

At the second level, calming dark grey acoustical fabric walls and carpet, coupled with luxurious fixed seating, enhance the experience of the demonstration theatre. Flanking the stairwell area are hardware and software displays, and a 'Genius' bar. The bar, display platforms, and seating throughout the store are solid, simply detailed maple tables and benches. Functional aspects of the store such as heating/cooling, lighting, security and acoustics are integrated into the design of, or hidden above, the crisp white stretched fabric of the ceiling system.

Throughout the space, rigorous attention to detail has created a 'static-free' environment. Distracting elements have been edited out of the visual field, making the magical experience of levitating on the stairs and bridge, while bathed in light from above, all the more dramatic. Simple, honest materials and thoughtfully resolved details echo qualities of the sophisticated, elegant computers and software on display.

completion	July 2002
client	Apple Computer Inc.
area	1670 square metres/18,000 square feet
materials	Glass, wood, stone, stainless steel frames
opposite	Front entry: a 1920's neo-classical structure, a former U.S. post office
top	Skylight, threaded by delicate stainless steel frames, admits abundant natural light
bottom	View of interior space from the street offers a compelling invitation
photography	Peter Aaron/Esto

awards	*Contract* magazine 2002
	Visual Merchandise and Store Design 2002
	AIA Pittsburgh Citation of Merit for
	Architectural Detail 2002
	AIA Pittsburgh Silver Medal for
	Architectural Design 2002
	AIA Pennsylvania Honor Award 2002
	Business Week/AIA Good Design is Good
	Business 2003
	Best of the Bay AIA San Francisco 2003
	AIA New York 2003
	SARA New York 2003
	Chicago Athenaeum 2003
opposite	Evening view
right	Inside, the eye is drawn to the levitating
	glass staircase, bridge and skylight system
bottom	Glass treads attract visitors upstairs, playing
	on the desire to 'walk on air'
photography	Peter Aaron/Esto

opposite left   Precisely connected metal inserts laminated into the glass contribute to visual weightlessness

opposite top   Top of the treads are diamond-plate fritted for safety and etched for modesty

opposite bottom   Store visitors enjoy walking and taking a break on the glass staircase

top   Depth of skylight well prevents glare from reaching computer screens below

bottom   Custom fixed seating enhances experience of product demonstration theatre

photography   Peter Aaron/Esto

Carlos Miele Flagship Store
Manhattan, New York, USA
Asymptote Architecture

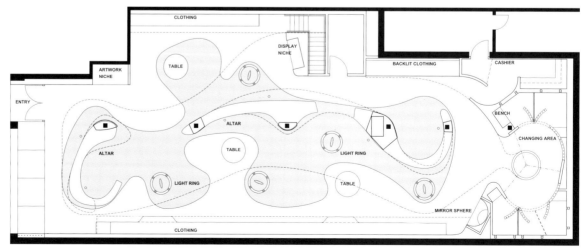

Asymptote's design for the Carlos Miele Flagship Store was conceived of as a bright open space, utilising a neutral palette of white and shades of pale green, green-blue and grey, all serving as foreground to Miele's colourful clothing design.

The interior space consists of two-tone, high-gloss epoxy flooring with embedded neon and halogen lighting, set beneath tempered glass rings. The curved, formed-steel hanging displays are cantilevered from the walls and sit above lacquered bent-plywood display units below. The storefront window display areas, as well as the circular change-rooms, utilise backlit floors and walls using 3M diffusion film, Plexiglas and fluorescent lighting. The contoured surface of the ceiling is formed from a high-gloss stretched PVC-based material produced by Barrisol.

The centrepiece of the store is a large floor-to-ceiling sculptural form that traverses the entire length of the interior space. This 'altar' element is used for both seating and display and is fabricated from lacquer-finished bent plywood over a rib and gusset sub-structure that was laser-cut directly from CAD drawings and fabricated off-site. Computer-generated drawings and digital procedures were also instrumental for both the design and fabrication of other curved forms and surfaces in the store.

Two 'Asymptote' video installations featuring digital art have been integrated into the architecture of the store, each piece celebrating an aspect of body and spatiality. These works are extensions of Asymptote's art projects recently included in Documenta XI and the Venice Biennale. The overall atmosphere of the space is shaped as much by the exuberant vivacity of Brazilian culture as it is by new technological means of fabrication, reflected in both the clothes and architectural elements. The environment is a deliberate insertion and provocation of not only the worlds of fashion, art and architecture but also a trans-urban meditation that merges the cultures of New York and São Paulo.

completion	June 2003
client	Carlos Miele
area	280 square metres/3000 square feet
materials	Two tone epoxy floor, Barrisol stretch fabric ceiling, roll-formed steel hanging units, illuminated Plexiglas walls, custom millwork: lacquered MDF skin applied over laser-cut MDF ribs
awards	*Contract* magazine Interior awards: Best Retail Project 2004 Best New York Retail 2004 Visual Merchandising and Retail Design
opposite top	Storefront view
opposite bottom	Floor plan
top and bottom	Interior views
photography	Paul Warchol

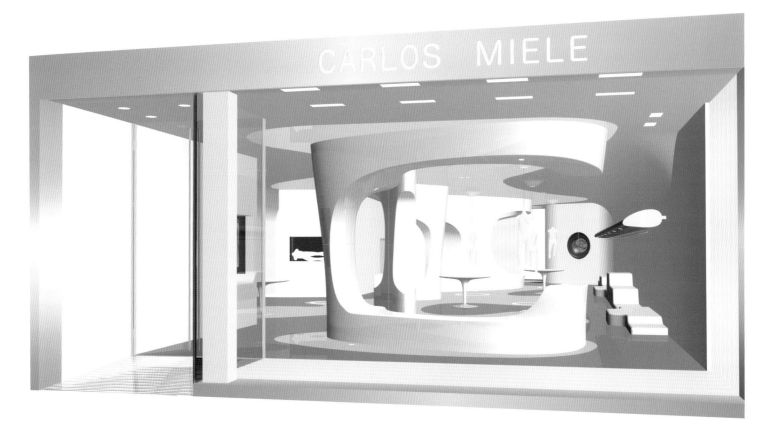

top   Altar rendering
bottom   Altar view from exterior
opposite   Altar view from interior
photography Paul Warchol

Cathedral of Our Lady of the Angels

Los Angeles, California, USA
Rafael Moneo

The new cathedral dominates its urban surroundings, emphasising its role as a landmark and spiritual centre. An esplanade for larger congregations of up to 6000 is at the centre of the site. A bell tower rises at the corner, and at the opposite end are the bishop's residence and facilities for the archdiocese. The visual focus of the exterior space is the Franciscan cross cut into the alabaster skylight of the cathedral façade.

The entrance to the cathedral is directly from the esplanade, through side doors into a perimeter corridor separated from the nave by outward-facing side chapels. The long, outer wall is without windows, so that it can be used for the stone plaques, inscriptions and votive offerings that will keep the history of the cathedral alive. To the west, opposite the presbytery, is the baptismal font. The corridor on the north side assumes a different character as the chapels look out onto the cloister garden, bringing them in contact with nature and the landscape of Los Angeles beyond. The nave with a capacity for 2000 worshippers, the main altar and pulpit flanked by tiers of seating, occupy the central longitudinal band of the cathedral. A large window with a cross dominates the altar area. The choir is placed beside the altar, pushed to the rear of the chancel in an open box above which rises the organ. The non-opaque façade surfaces behind the organ consist of alabaster louvres that create a second focus of filtered light in the altar area. The same alabaster louvres are used for the large windows of the nave's lateral façade. The light filtered through the alabaster creates a luminous, diffuse and enveloping atmosphere, not unlike that experienced in Byzantine churches.

completion	2002
client	Archdiocese of Los Angeles
area	21,150 square metres/235,000 square feet (site area)
	4000 square metres/56,765 square feet (cathedral)
materials	Sand-blasted concrete, Spanish alabaster in aluminium mullions, Spanish limestone, suspended ceiling of fir and hemlock
cost	USD$193.5 million (total project cost)
opposite	View from highway
right	Cloister garden and campanile
photography	Duccio Malagamba

left, below and bottom   Cathedral interiors
photography   Duccio Malagamba

City Center and City 2 Shopping Mall
Brussels, Belgium
Atelier d'Art Urbain

Completed in the 1920s, the former Bon Marché department store in central Brussels forms part of the urban memory and has been rebuilt and transformed into City Center. At the request of the Monuments Commission, the Bon Marché's characteristic Art Deco façade was restored and preserved. The client wanted the spirit of the Bon Marché façade to be reflected in the new façade of the building above the City 2 Shopping Mall entrance, giving the appearance of a large building with an homogeneous appearance on the boulevard.

City Center comprises offices organised around two glass-roofed atriums, retail shops at ground level and parking spaces. Together with the renovated City 2 Shopping Mall, City Center is probably the largest mixed-used ensemble built in more than 30 years in the centre of the capital of Europe. Five-storey housing has been included at the rear of the project, and this, together with the urban treatment of the entire façade, has completed the urban renewal at this strategic location.

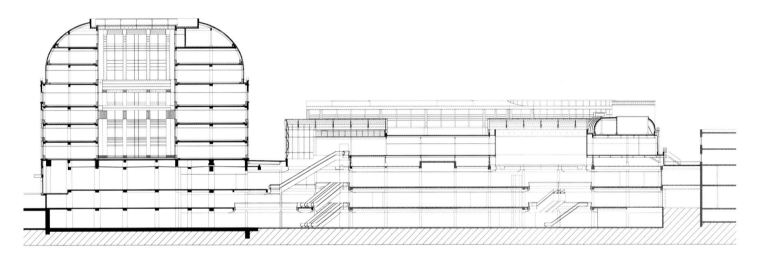

completion	June 2003
co-architect	Design Architectural (shopping mall interiors)
client	Fortis Real Estate
area	100,000 square metres/1,076,000 square feet
structure	Concrete; steel for the shopping mall penthouse level
materials	Natural stone, powder-coated aluminium
opposite	Main City 2 Shopping Mall entrance
photography	Marc Detiffe
top	General view of City Center offices showing the preserved 1928 façade integrated in the project
middle	Section showing the City Center offices to left and City 2 Shopping Mall on right
right	City Center offices main lobby
photography	Yvan Glavie

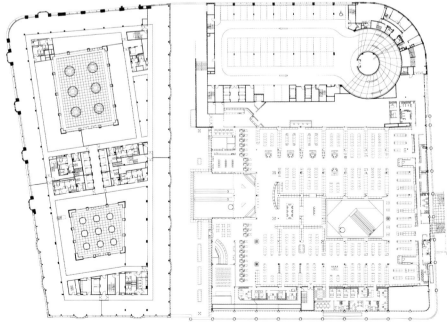

opposite top   City Center housing corner façade
opposite left   Atrium in City Center office building
photography   Yvan Glavie
opposite right   Atrium in City 2 Shopping Mall
photography   Marc Detiffe
top   General view from Place Rogier
photography   Yvan Glavie
right   Floor plans showing a typical office level,
the Fnac department store level above the
City 2 Shopping Mall, a garage level and a
housing level

Giorgio Armani Store
London, UK
Claudio Silvestrin

The Giorgio Armani store in London is the latest in a series of flagship stores around the world.

The choice of materials, the design of the entrance hall and staircases, the use of natural light and the fluidity of the space are all characteristic features of the design concept. The articulated and sophisticated ensemble of the design features brings a timeless atmosphere to the store. The materials are few, precious, natural and ancient.

The floor and the walls are clad in St Maximin limestone, the furniture in Macassar ebony and oxidised brass.

The entrance hall is always a poetic pause, a threshold between the exterior and the retail zone. Often, water is the symbolic element that makes this space magical – for the London store, the symbolic feature at the entrance is intentionally more potent than ever, reminiscent of sacred and archaic sites.

completion	September 2003
area	1000 square metres/10,760 square feet
opposite top	View of store from street
opposite bottom	View of stairs from entrance zone
top	View of void
above	Curved corridor with display niches
photography	James Morris

Hotel Unique

São Paulo, Brazil
Ruy Ohtake – Arquitetura e Urbanismo

With its unique shape, the hotel makes an architectural statement in the midst of urban São Paulo. An inverted arch, it is supported at each end by a massive concrete pier. The resulting 25-metre-high curved voids house the main hotel entrance on the right side and the conference hall and restaurant entrance on the left. The 1.8-metre-diameter circular windows are a dynamic feature of the façade, and are accentuated by the pre-rusted copper plaque in three shades of green.

The six-level hotel has 96 rooms. The lobby, bar and administration areas are located in a dramatic, double-height area on the ground level, which also features a wide transparent glass wall that allows interaction between the hotel lobby and the streets of São Paulo. The beige marble walls, white furnishings, and transparent glass tables and fittings of the lobby increase the sensations of light and space. The roof-top restaurant has the same glass detailing and metallic structure, opening the whole space to panoramic views of the city, while the roof-top swimming pool is a spectacular study in red. The conference hall, located in the first underground level, incorporates modular rooms, and can accommodate up to 1500 people. Three further underground levels accommodate parking facilities and other hotel infrastructure.

The qualities of the internal space are similar to the external – the apartment corridors are curved, drawing in natural light. The corner rooms feature curved floors, similar to the façade design, rising up to meet the roof, forming unexpected spaces.

completion	2002
area	20,500 square metres/220,700 square feet
materials	Concrete, glass, copper, wood
awards	Master Prize 2003/FIABCI/SECOVI Architectonics Solutions – Prominence in Architecture
opposite top left	Hotel lobby and bar
opposite top right	Lobby
opposite bottom	General view
top	Lobby
middle	Corner apartment with curved floor
bottom	Rooftop swimming pool
photography	Nelson Kon

The JCC in Manhattan
New York, New York, USA
Diamond and Schmitt Architects Incorporated

The program for the Jewish Community Center, on Manhattan's Upper West Side is complex, involving three main sectors of activity: cultural and educational facilities with 12 special classrooms, an auditorium, a nursery school for 150 children and a 'biet midrash' religious study space with meeting rooms and a library; a fitness centre with a 25-metre training pool, a regulation size gymnasium, aerobics studios and exercise equipment studios; and general administrative and special programs offices.

The architectural design for the Centre is conceived as a lantern or a beacon reaching out to the surrounding community. The 9-storey building (plus three levels below grade) is clad in glass with a high degree of transparency between inside activities and the street.

As a result of the small urban site, the most difficult aspect of the design was the vertical organisation of the complex program. The stacking of different program elements added a great deal of technical complexity to mechanical and electrical systems, and made the cohesive legibility of the building more challenging. To assist with legibility, each of the three sectors of activity were linked internally as coherent units.

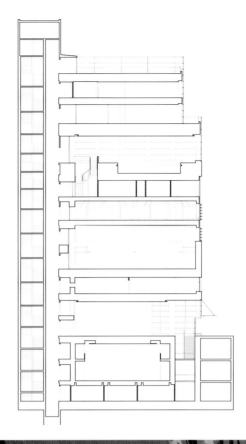

completion	May 2002
client	Jewish Community Centre
area	11,150 square metres/120,000 square feet
structure	Manganese Ironspot brick (SW grade FBX Norman size) non glazed, chosen for its 'severe weathering' capabilities to accommodate the harsh New York environment
cost	CAD$74,260,000
awards	Canadian Architect Award of Excellence 2000
opposite	Exterior, corner of Amsterdam and 76th Streets
top	Section
bottom	Main entrance on Amsterdam street
photography	Steven Evans

opposite	View of café from street
top left	Stairs from lobby to lower levels
top right	Library
bottom	Lobby on main level
photography	Steven Evans

opposite   Aquatics centre on 5th floor
top   Pool plan
bottom   Roof-top terrace and playground
photography   Steven Evans

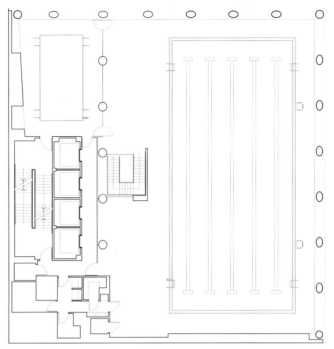

AC Martin Partners, Inc.
444 South Flower Street, Suite 1200
Los Angeles, California, 90071
USA
Tel: +1 213 683 1900 Fax: +1 213 614 6002
www.acmartin.com

Aleks Istanbullu Architects
1659 11th Street, Suite 200
Santa Monica, California, 90404
USA
Tel: +1 310 450 8246 Fax: +1 310 399 1888
www.ai-architects.com

Architects Design Group, Inc
333 North Knowles Avenue
Winter Park, Florida, 32789
USA
Tel: +1 407 647 1706 Fax: +1 407 645 5525
www.architectsdesigngroup.com

Assar
Chaussée de La Hulpe 181
B-1170, Brussels
Belgium
Tel: +32 2 672 6824 Fax: +32 2 672 8337
www.assar.com

Asymptote Architecture
561 Broadway, Suite 5A
New York, New York, 10012
USA
Tel: +1 212 343 7333 Fax: +1 212 343 7099
www.asymptote.net

Atelier d'Art Urbain
Avenue Brugmann 16
B-1060 Brussels
Belgium
Tel: +32 2 673 0779 Fax: +32 2 672 0957
www.atelier-art-urbain.com

Atelier Hitoshi Abe;
Hitoshi Abe, Yasuaki Onoda
3-3-16 Oroshimachi
Wakabayashi-Ku
Sendai, Mayagi
Japan
Tel: +81 22 284 3411 Fax: +81 22 782 1233
www.a-slash.jp

Augustin und Frank Architekten
Schlesische Strasse 29-30
10997 Berlin
Germany
Tel: +49 612 843 57/58 Fax: +49 612 843 59
www.augustinundfrank.de

Behnisch, Behnisch & Partner
Christophstrasse 6,
70178 Stuttgart
Germany
Tel: +49 711 607 720 Fax: +49 711 607 7299
www.behnisch.com

Bernard Tschumi Architects
227 West 17th Street
New York, New York, 10011
USA
Tel: +1 212 807 6340 Fax: +1 212 242 3693
www.tschumi.com

Bohlin Cywinski Jackson
1932 First Avenue, Suite 916
Seattle, Washington, 98101
USA
Tel: +1 206 256 0862 Fax: +1 206 256 0864
www.bcj.com

Charles Rose Architects Inc
115 Willow Avenue
Somerville, Massachusetts, 02144
USA
Tel: +1 617 628 5033 Fax: +1 617 628 7033
www.charlesrosearchitects.com

Architects

Christian de Portzamparc
1, rue de l'Aude
Paris, 75014
France
Tel: +33 1 4064 8000
www.chdeportzamparc.com

Claudio Silvestrin Architects
Unit 18
44–48 Wharf Road, Waterside
London, N1 7UX
UK
Tel: +44 20 7490 7797 Fax: +44 20 7490 727
www.claudiosilvestrin.com

Daly Genik Architects
1558 10th St C
Santa Monica, California, 90401
USA
Tel: +1 310 656 3180 Fax: +1 310 656 3183
www.dalygenik.com

**Diamond and Schmitt Architects
Incorporated**
2 Berkeley Street
Toronto, Ontario M5A 2W3
Canada
Tel: +1 416 862 8800 Fax: +1 416 862 5508
www.dsai.ca

Du Besset–Lyon architectes
30 Rue Ligner
75020 Paris
France
Tel: +33 1 4367 1675 Fax : +33 1 4367 1600
www.dubesset-lyon.com

**EDH+MIAS;
Masaki Endoh + Masahiro Ikeda**
2-13-8, Honnmachi, Shibuya-ku
Tokyo, 151-0071
Japan
Tel: +81 3 3377 6293 Fax : +81 3 3377 6293
edh-endoh@mvi.biglobe.ne.jp

Elliott + Associates Architects
35 Harrison Avenue
Oklahoma City, Oklahoma, 73104
USA
Tel: +1 405 232 9554 Fax : +1 405 232 9997
www.e-a-a.com

Foster and Partners
Riverside Three
22 Hester Road
London SW11 4AN
UK
Tel: +44 20 7738 0455 Fax: + 44 20 7738 1107
www.fosterandpartners.com

Gehry Partners LLP
12541 Beatrice Street
Los Angeles, California, 90066
USA
Tel: +1 310 482 3000 Fax: +1 310 482 3006
keithm@FOGA.com

Gould Evans
3135 N. 3rd Avenue
Phoenix, Arizona, 85013
USA
Tel: +1 602 234 1140 Fax: +1 602 234 1156
www.gouldevans.com

Gullichsen Vormala Architects
Pursimiehenkatu 29 A
00150 Helsinki
Finland
Tel: +358 9 686 9300 Fax: +358 9 6869 3050
architects@gullichsen-vormala.fi

Heikkinen-Komonen Architects
Kristianinkatu 11–13
00170 Helsinki
Finland
Tel: +358 9 75102 111 Fax: +358 9 75102 166
www.heikkinen-komonen.fi

Joseph Wong Design Associates (JWDA)
2359 Fourth Avenue, Suite 300
San Diego, California, 92101
USA
Tel: +1 619 233 6777 Fax: +1 619 237 0541
www.jwdainc.com

Juhani Katainen Architects
Töölönkatu 12 A 14
FI 00111 Helsinki
Finland
Tel: +358 9 440 231 Fax: +358 9 496 539
juhani.katainen@kolumbus.fi

Koen van Velsen
Spoorstraat 69a
1211 GA Hilversum
Netherlands
Tel: +31 35 622 2000 Fax: +31 35 628 8991
kvv@architecten.A2000.nl

Lab architecture studio
Level 4, 325 Flinders Lane
Melbourne, Victoria, 3000
Australia
Tel: +61 3 9612 1026 Fax: +61 3 9620 3088
www.labarchitecture.com

Machado and Silvetti Associates
560 Harrison Avenue
Boston, Massachusetts, 02118
USA
Tel: +1 617 426 7070 Fax: +1 617 426 3604
www.machado-silvetti.com

Mansilla + Tuñón Architects
Ríos Rosas 11, 6º
28003 Madrid
Spain
Tel/Fax: +34 1 913 993 067
circo@circo.e.telefonica.net

MCA – Mario Cucinella Architects
Via Matteotti 21
40129 Bologna
Italy
Tel: +39 51 631 3381 Fax: +39 51 631 3316
www.mcarchitects.it

Murphy/Jahn, Inc.
35 East Wacker Drive
Chicago, Illinois, 60601
USA
Tel: +1 312 427 7300 Fax: +1 312 332 0274
www.murphyjahn.com

MVRDV
Dunantstraat 10
Postbus 63136
3002 JC Rotterdam
Netherlands
Tel: +31 10 477 2860 Fax: +31 10 466 3627
www.mvrdv.archined.nl/mvrdv.html

NBBJ
111 South Jackson Street
Seattle, Washington, 98104
USA
Tel: +1 310 448 9601 Fax: +1 310 448 9900
www.nbbj.com

Neutelings Riedijk Architecten
Scheepmakersstraat 15–17
NL–3011 VH Rotterdam
Netherlands
Tel: +31 10 404 66 77 Fax: +31 10 414 27 12
info@neutelings-riedijk.com

Pasanella + Klein Stolzman + Berg Architects
330 West 42nd Street
New York, New York, 10036
USA
Tel: +1 212 594 2010 Fax: +1 212 947 4381
www.pksb.com

**Paula Gutierrez Erlandsen –
Arquitectura y Decoración**
Don Carlos 3171, Las Condes
Santiago
Chile
Tel: +56 2 231 5564
www.paulagutierrez.com

Pugh + Scarpa
Bergamot Station
2525 Michigan Avenue, Building F1
Santa Monica, California, 90404
USA
Tel: +1 310 828 0226 Fax: +1 310 453 9606
www.pugh-scarpa.com

Rafael Moneo
Cinca 5
28002 Madrid,
Spain
Tel: +34 915 642 257 Fax: +34 915 635 217

Rafael Viñoly Architects
50 Vandam Street
New York, New York, 10013
USA
Tel: +1 212 924 5060 Fax: +1 212 924 5858
www.rvapc.com

Renzo Piano Building Workshop
via P.P. Rubens, 29
16158 Genova
Italy
Tel: +39 10 6171 1 Fax: +39 10 6171 350
www.rpwf.org

Ruy Ohtake – Arquitetura e Urbanismo
Avenida Faria Lima 1597 11º andar
São Paulo
SP Brazil
Tel: +55 11 3094 8009 Fax: +55 11 3814 1888
www.ruyohtake.com.br

Saucier + Perrotte Architects
110 Rue Jean Talon Ouest
Montreal, Quebec, H2R 2X1
Canada
Tel: +1 514 273 1700 Fax: +1 514 273 3501
www.saucierperrotte.com

Sauerbruch Hutton Architects
Lehrter Strasse 57
10557 Berlin
Germany
Tel: +49 30 3978 21-0 Fax: +49 30 3978 2130
www.sauerbruchhutton.com

space international inc.
5727 Venice Boulevard
Los Angeles, California, 90019
USA
Tel: +1 323 954 9084 Fax: +1 323 954 9085
www.space-intl.com

Stephen Jolson Architects
Studio 1/251 Chapel Street
Prahran, Victoria, 3181
Australia
Tel: +61 3 9533 7997 Fax: +61 3 9533 7978
stephen@sjarchitect.com

The Manser Practice
Bridge Studios
Hammersmith Bridge
London, W6 9DA
UK
Tel: +44 20 8741 4381 Fax: +44 20 8741 2773
www.manser.co.uk

Woods Bagot
Level 13, Waterfront Place
1 Eagle Street
Brisbane, Queensland, 4001
Australia
Tel: +61 7 3221 3122 Fax: +61 7 3221 3022
www.woodsbagot.com

Zaha Hadid Architects
Studio 9, 10 Bowling Green Lane
London EC1R OBQ
UK
Tel: +44 20 7253 5147 Fax: +44 20 7251 8322
www.zaha-hadid.com

The information and illustrations in this publication have been prepared and supplied by the contributors. While all reasonable efforts have been made to ensure accuracy, the publishers do not, under any circumstances, accept responsibility for errors, omissions and representations expressed or implied.